#VETERANSLIKEUS:

PTSD Symptoms In Combat Veterans

by Sere Wilde

Published 2019

About the Author

Between 1963 to 1972, the US Army train 12,000 lieutenants to lead infantry platoons for combat in Vietnam. Some graduate from the West Point Military Academy. Others graduate from the 23 week Officer Candidate School at Ft. Benning, Georgia.

Others, like me, got their Reserve Officer Training Corp commissions directly upon graduation from college after attending training in the summer months and continuing through the college years. 6,598 Officers are killed in Vietnam.

I graduate from college in the middle of the Vietnam War. Almost immediately, I ams called to Active Duty to begin my two year tour of duty.

#Veteranslikeus: PTSD Symptoms In Combat Soldiers are some of my experiences in Vietnam. And some of my Stateside experiences since returning from Vietnam

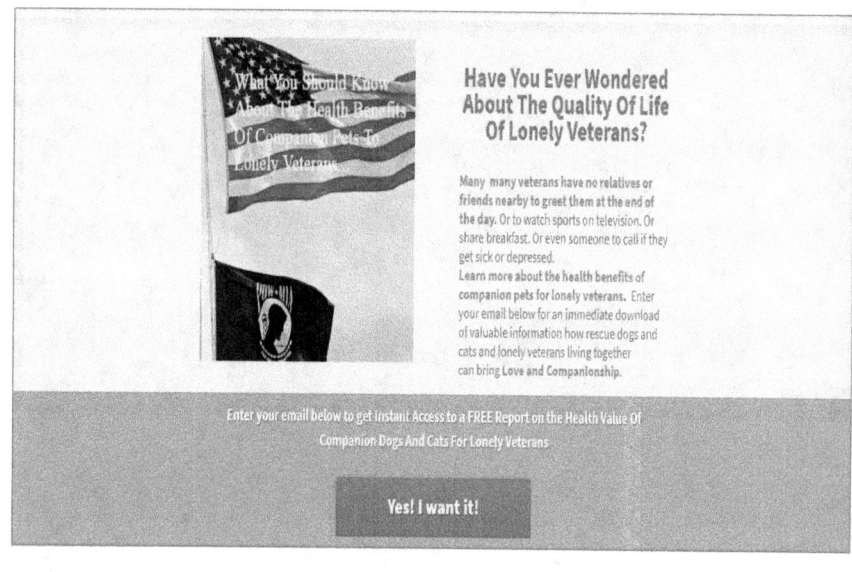

And if you feel like you want to help improve the quality of life for a lonely Veteran, visit https://companions.lpages.co/many-veterans-have-no-friends/ **to see how you can help …**

God and the soldier, we adore
In time of danger, not before.
The danger past and all things righted,
God's forgotten, the soldier slighted.
- Rudyard Kipling -

2.69 million American men and women serve in Vietnam.

Of that number, 15% …at any given time …have the job of "trigger-puller. Someone whose job is to put North Vietnamese Army troops into their sights and pull the trigger. Many are door-gunners on helicopters ferrying troops into combat.

Others are Forward Observers calling in artillery fire on North Vietnamese Army positions. Quite a few are infantrymen carrying machine guns and M-16's. Aviators fly endless "Puff'" the Magic Dragon missions armed with its multiple machine guns. Others sight the enemy from the turret of a tank.

PROLOGUE

"#Veteranslikeus: PTSD Symptoms In Combat Soldiers makes me smile, laugh, hurt and cry. You are painting a picture of war that few people have or will ever experience. It is important that you do this. I hope that these writings find their way to a larger audience than those of us privileged few who are experiencing them. War, to this generation, is a fictional activity, confined to movies and video games.

Many of my students, when I was teaching high school, were intrigued by Vietnam and could only see what they thought was the glory and "coolness" of combat. The most asked question was "Did you ever kill anyone?" What bothered me was the way the question was asked, like wow, you were really cool if you had actually killed another human being. I thank God I was never put in the position where I had to.Their impressions were reinforced by the media coverage of Desert Storm, in which war was portrayed as a sterile video game like experience.

I hope however, that you can find some way to publish #Veteranslikeus: PTSD Symptoms In Combat Soldiers in print also. This generation, and future generations need to hear not only your experiences but they need to hear your feelings and get even just a small glimpse of your hurt, fear and emotion. I know they will probably not be able to fully understand all they will read or hear, but even if they get just one small percentage point of understanding, they and society as a whole, will be the better for it."

-A Vietnam Veteran -

INTRODUCTION

Some time ago, somebody that I knew for 25 years said to me " ... I do not believe it's good for you to tell and in some cases repeat your story. Each time I hear your story it (to me) seems that you become more depressed. I believe it is time for you to leave your story behind and move on."

"... you and your 5 veterans are still living in the past. If you still need to tell your story, my question would be "how long do you need to keep telling your story?"

The pages that follow answer that question.

There is room enough for all shades of opinion on the Vietnam experience. I thought so when I was in Vietnam. I think so now.

As for those weary of our stories, tell us "Where the hell were you?"

It is Monday. You have another 9:00 appointment with a specialist in treating hatred and phobias. You also have your regular 3:00 group meeting with fellow PTSD vets. It is easier on all concerned if you just stay at Ft. Miley all day instead of traveling back and forth.

Of course, if you drove...

So you spend your time wandering over the hospital grounds. You go buy a cup of chocolate in the cafeteria. You go sit in "Assessments & Evaluations" (Emergency Room). You go over to Building 8 (Psych Building) and sit downstairs in the waiting room.

Ultimately getting bored of this little dance, you sit in the lobby of the Main Entrance and people watch. The Residents from UC-San Francisco Med School in their white coats, stethoscopes tossed around their neck and over their shoulder and walk at a fast pace. You watch the aged father struggling up the ramp with his cane ... as his wife and grown-up daughter walk behind him encouraging his every step.

As he enters Building 208, you and others notice that he is wearing a gold-and-white braided cap that says "Bataan Death March Survivor". Conversations in the lobby stop. People crowded around the Information Desk instantly part so that he has a barrier free corridor to walk through.

Conversation resumes as the Filipino veteran disappears down the hallway.

A furiously angry vet comes running out of the Assessments and Evaluations. He stops at the Information Desk and profanely cusses out at the clerk sitting there about the two hour wait he has endured to get his meds.

Which he still doesn't have.

Wheelchair vet rumbles down the hallway. He is missing his right leg. He stops in front of your chair and wheels around to watch others coming and going out of the Main Entrance. 10 minutes later, he puts his hands on the wheels, spins around and looks you directly in the eyes. You return his stare with a smile. His body softens as he returns your smile.

You think that you can't do this on Monday's anymore.

So you walk down the hallway to the Cafeteria.

There is a crowd around the ATM machine. A vet with two hooks for hands is feverishly trying to extract a dollar bill from his wallet for the Coke machine next to the ATM. You offer to help. He says "Just give me a moment, I can do this". Finally he does so.

You continue on to the Cafeteria.

Your stomach goes berserk. A scream begins at your toes and rises to your throat like a volcano about to explode. You feel a need to pound a fist through the walls. It takes every iota of willpower that you got not to scream at the top of your lungs. Tears flow until you remember to take a deep breath. Everything will be OK. Just take a deep deep breath.

You will be here next Monday.

Just like you were here last Monday.

And then one day there won't be any more Monday's.

You will be home with those you loved ... those who will always be forever young ... with their names etched on a Wall in Washington DC.

Thank you America.

Chapter 1

The sole purpose is to give the viewer an insight of what it is like to live with PTSD on a day-to-day basis.

My personal medical file at the VA: "**Subject has occupational and social impairment, with deficiencies in most areas, such as work, school, family relations, judgment, thinking, or mood, due to such symptoms as: suicidal ideation; obsessional rituals which interfere with routine activities; speech is intermittently illogical, obscure, or irrelevant; near-continuous panic or depression affecting the ability to function independently, appropriately and effectively; impaired impulse control (such as unprovoked irritability with periods of violence); spatial disorientation; neglect of personal appearance and hygiene; difficulty in adapting to stressful circumstances (including work or a work like setting); and an inability to establish and maintain effective relationships**".

Each of us who served in combat and is suffering from PTSD is somebody's son whose life expectancy is shorter than the national average, has a higher risk for neurological and cardiology problems and whose social skills are lacking in the common courtesies.

This story needs to be told so that it won't ever happen again. I hope viewers will think carefully about what it really means when the recruiting ads shout "An Army of One". Thank you!

Sere:

For what it is worth, the following incident is among the kind that my Father reluctantly agreed to hear about for the first time ...six months ago. My 42 year brother pretends that it never happened and Stephanie learned about three years ago. Even though it has been more than 30 years since it occurred. It has been my experience and that of fellow vets that most people don't know and/or don't want to know what really happens in combat.

This incident is one of the most common in my mind whether I am working, relaxing, reading or sleeping.

My battalion has the mission of detecting, identifying and ultimately destroying NVA troop concentrations in the "Parrot's Beak" area along the Cambodian border. These seasoned NVA troops from the 324-A Regiment and the 324-B Regiment usually come across the border at night varying in strength from squad (about 11 people) to battalion size (about 600) in the effort to join other regular NVA units in completing their encirclement of Saigon.

My specific function as platoon leader is closing in clandestinely on NVA units that had just crossed over the border into South Vietnam and, by means of stealth, ambush, deception and long-range sniper teams, capture or kill those NVA personnel that appear to be in positions of leadership.

My first "contact" with the NVA took place several days after I joined my unit in the field. There were 17 men, mostly volunteers, and one "Chiu-¹Hoi" who was intimately familiar with the rice paddy terrain that we were operating in. A "Chiu-Hoi" is a Viet Cong or North Vietnamese Army soldier who changes sides to fight with us against their former comrades.

It was getting close to sundown and we had not run into any NVA during the 2 or 3 days that we had been on patrol. I got a radio message (from our S3-Operations Officer) that we were going to be extracted within the next 20 minutes and sent to another location to perform an ambush along a canal. Being new to this area, I asked for a couple minutes to confirm our specific coordinates for the 3 "slicks" (gunship/helicopter) inbound to our location.

I passed the information to my men who then spread out in a circle and then motioned the "Chiu-Hoi" to join me alongside a berm to confirm our location. I placed my map on the ground and put my thumb on the location where we were located. He squatted down, looked at the map and then turned his head to face me.

The next thing I knew was that my world went black. I couldn't see or breathe. Reaching up to my face, I felt bone fragments and wet and messy flesh covering me from the neck up. The "Chiu-Hoi" had taken a round in the back of his head and it had exited through his chin. Wiping my face with my towel, I kept gagging and throwing up from his brain tissue that I had swallowed.

No other rounds came in as we threw out a smoke grenade to mark our location for the incoming "slicks".

I reported the incident via radio to the S-3 when we landed at our new ambush location. For several days afterward, I couldn't eat without throwing up.

We left the "Chiu-Hoi" there. He deserved better.

Chapter 2

Hi All:

A lot of things going on since my last update. So let's get started. First I have decided to change the working title from VIETNAM: A PTSD PERSPECTIVE to #Veteranslikeus: PTSD Symptoms In Combat Soldiers .

I now have over 133 pages of notes, book reviews, transcripts of speeches, audio recordings, photographs, government documents, draft statistics, psychiatric studies, magazine abstracts and more related strictly to Vietnam PTSD. The majority of research is now completed.

Next on the agenda is locating 3 combat Viet Vets with certain qualifications: a Vietnam Veteran operating room nurse, a wife whose husband meets the criteria of the DD-214 and a 50% or more veterans disability pension and a 10 to 14 year child of a Vietnam Vet willing to speak of their experiences on camera.

I do have a couple of leads on the combat Vets but none on the wife or the nurse or young child. If I can't find a nurse, I will look for a parent of a Vet.

Next week, I should have completed an 8½ by 11 inch brochure inviting potential interview subjects to contact me directly.

Just so you know that a little humor lightens a heavy subject, I came across this the other day.

A Vietnam Vet jumps into the dark night from a C-130 airplane, lands in the bush at 0245, night moves 10 miles with a 55 pound pack, 15 pound weapon, basic combat-load ammo and when he views the NVA says, "Man, this is the shit..."

A Navy Seal helicopters behind the lines, swims 5 miles to his objective, converts to land and does a 10 mile night movement, with 50 pounds of gear, 15 pound weapon, fighting knife and upon seeing the NVA says, "Man, this is some deep shit...."

A Marine is forced to land 15 miles farther away from his objective due to bad weather. He makes up the time by double-timing 24 miles in broad daylight, with a 60 pound pack, 15 pound weapon, hunting knife, extra ammo, must dispatch three NVA with his hands enroute and upon viewing his objective finally says, "Man, I love this shit....

"An Air Force Airman sits in his dress blue uniform, coffee in hand, stereo playing Johnny Cash, air-conditioned trailer just above freezing only to just find out he has been scheduled for KP duty and will miss the Robert Hope show and says, "Man, what kinda shit is this?"

Producing a 75 to 90 minute documentary on this subject comes with a number of unexpected surprises. Not all of them to my liking. For instance, earlier tonight I was doing research on the snakes we frequently encountered. Cobras, kraits, one-steppers, two-steppers and the like.

When the computer screen filled up with all the references, I got an immediate chill that I couldn't shake. Some much so that I had to turn the computer off and go and try and get warm.

Finally, I told Stephanie what was going on and she said to rub her back. That usually distracts me but it only did for about 45 minutes.

I went to bed at 1:00 am and it is now 5:00 am and I still feel that chill. I carried a Smith & Wesson .38 with silencer and one of its uses was for dispatching snakes without alerting the whole universe that we were in the area. I hate snakes!!! Hate snakes!!! Hate snakes to this day!!!

And the NVA don't like them any better than we did.

Since this documentary is viewed from the perspective of the combat vet with PTSD, I feel it is important for the viewer to have an accurate view of what life was like in the field including living conditions and hazards to one's health other than the NVA. It is very difficult, if not impossible, to show temperatures in the 100's on film, the lack of regular sleep, mosquito swarms at night, the pollution upstream from the irrigations ditches where we get our water, the endless variety of unknown insects, leeches from flooded rice paddies, canals and the like or the regular cycles of constipation and diarrhea that affect us all.

Perhaps you can help.

In my closing narration, I want to emphasize how the viewer can help the veteran and his family.

Words of wisdom learned the hard way:
A Purple Heart just proves that were you smart enough to think of a plan, stupid enough to try it, and lucky enough to survive.

Sere

.

Chapter 3

Research indicates the majority of combat and non-combat vets DO NOT talk about their military experiences ... except in a most general way. If they do talk to each other, it is along the lines of "What branch were you in?" "Did you enlist of get drafted?" "Where did you go through Basic Training?"

And that is about it ...for an experience that took 2 to 4 years out of their life.

Walking the hallways or eating in the cafeteria at Ft. Miley (VA hospital), I frequently overhear conversations between vets who don't know each other ...and are going to their next appointments. Some are missing body parts. Some are missing minds. And some are missing both.

You are a civilian if:

You can call your boss Mike. Also, you can call in sick without having to go see a medic

You make full use of both arms for carrying items. And save loads of time not looking for your hat.

You have finally worked "Airborne", "Air Assault", "Shit!", and "Fuck" out of your daily vocabulary.

Business lunches, golfing, and 49er season tickets are considered an essential part of work.

The ability to run long distances quickly and do many push-ups or sit-ups is not confused for intelligence, leadership potential, or degree of motivation.

You have determined brown T-shirts and olive drab socks go with nothing in the real world.

The office empties at 5:15 PM. The only people left behind are ex-military whose wives can't take the shock of seeing their spouses before 7:00 PM.

There are no guards at the entrance to your subdivision.

Jumping out of a perfectly good plane on a business trip is considered a federal offense.

Making a documentary for broadcast TV and, perhaps, theatrical distribution is very tedious regarding the details. What kind of film (or video) to record on? Can I get copyright clearance to use that photograph or audio recording? How can I ask the interviewee questions and still operate the camera at the same time? What kinds of people would watch this documentary and what is the best (read: cheapest) way to reach them? Where can I get some studio lights and backdrops (cheap)? Why has no one done this type of documentary before? What can I put into the documentary to move the viewer to take action to talk with veterans in his/her own family or community of friends, co-workers, and neighbors?

Seeking answers to these questions and more keeps me up nights, weekends, holidays.

Now you can be in-the-know around the water cooler with the slang used in Vietnam. However, watch out for that old coot in the office who keeps to himself.

A duffle bag drag and a bowl of corn flakes:

The final meal at Ton Son Nhut Air Force Base prior to boarding the Big Bird for the flight back to the land of the big PX.

AK-47: Basic infantry rifle of the NVA.

The AK-47 was the basic infantry weapon of the North Vietnamese Army (NVA) and the Vietcòng (VC). Originally manufactured by the Soviet Union, most these "Assault rifles" used in the war were made in the People's Republic of China, which was the major supplier of armaments to NVA and VC forces.

Also known as the Kalishnikov, after its Russian inventor, this weapon was sturdy, reliable, compact, and relatively lightweight. It fires a 7.62mm bullet in a fully automatic mode. Its high velocity and tumbling action of the bullet contribute to its effectiveness. The combination of these effects plus its rapid-fire capability means that accuracy is not a major requirement, thus reducing the training time before a soldier could be sent into combat.

Most armament experts judge the AK-47, which normally holds thirty bullets, to be a superior weapon compared to the U.S. M-16. In fact, this is my preferred weapon despite its distinctive "popping" sound that jittery troops might mistake for the enemy.

AMNESTY BOX: a bright blue box made of solid steel shaped like a free-standing US Postal box. It sands in the Travis Air Force Base in front of the customs line so you could dump any contraband (drugs, weapons, porn magazines, whatever) no questions asked, before going through customs.

ARVN: Army of South Vietnam.

B-52 BOMBER: The B-52 is regarded by experts as the most successful military aircraft ever produced. .

B-52's used in Vietnam/Afghanistan/Iraq carry eighty-four 500-pound bombs internally and twenty-four 750 pound bombs non-stop for a 3,000-mile mission.

The first B-52 raids against a target in South Vietnam (and the first war action for the B-52) took place on June 18, 1965. The target was a Vietcong jungle sanctuary. The results were not encouraging. Two B-52s collided in flight to the target and were lost in the Pacific Ocean. The results of the bombing could not be evaluated because the area was controlled by the Viet Cong.

B-52s were called in to disrupt enemy troop concentrations and supply areas with devastating effect. They flew 124,532 sorties. Thirty-one B-52s were lost: during the war.

BATTALION: (Bn) a battalion is an organizational institution in the Army and Marine Corps. Commanded by a lieutenant colonel, an infantry battalion usually has around 900 people and an artillery battalion about 500 people.

During the Vietnam War, American battalions were usually much half that size and expected to accomplish the same results as a full strength unit.

Questions and Answers:

Q. What do you hope to accomplish with the documentary?

A. My goal is for the viewer to understand just how the PTSD experience drastically impacts the veteran's life forever.

Q. Is there a political slant?

A. The emphasis within the documentary are the real human beings who are still fighting the war. And the families, friends and neighbors who are caught up fighting the war with them.

Q. How has your family encouraged you along the way?

My wife Stephanie has been most supportive in every way that she can...even when I am driving her nuts!! My oldest son, Robert, is doing the research for the snakes. My younger son, Daniel is going to drive me to the interview sites as well as operate the Sony camcorder. .

Words of wisdom learned the hard way:

Depending upon the urgency of the tactical situation, always cradle a rapidly dying soldier until he stops screaming/gurgling/twitching and goes limp.

Nobody should die; alone, in the dirt... 9,000 miles from home.

Sere

Chapter 4

Vietnam Pop Quiz:

1.   What was the name of the Secretary of Defense during the troop build-up in Vietnam?

2.   Who was the 80 year Selective Service Director?

3.   Who was the Commander of US forces in Vietnam?

4.   What does POW mean?

5.   Who was the Secretary of State that was awarded the Nobel Peace Price for negotiating the end of direct US involvement in Vietnam hostilities?

6.   What was the capitol of South Vietnam?

7.   What does NVA mean?

8.   Who was the Vietnamese revolutionary that successfully fought the Japanese, the French and later the US?

Recently, I received a letter from my Dad telling me that "he could not support my documentary". And that furthermore "It is over, over there. It is a dead issue". Senator McCain's recent comments about "gooks" indicates that it may be over, over there in Vietnam but it isn't over, over here in the United States.

Last year, 4.7 million visitors came to the Vietnam Veterans Memorial Wall in Washington DC. I bring this item up only to illustrate the divisions about Vietnam that still separate us.

My experience was that the Viet Cong (Vietnamese Communist) were commonly referred to as "Victor Charlie" or "Mr. Sere" or "Charlie". The NVA are simply NVA. This distinction is important because "Charlie" usually hits your very hard and then runs for cover.

The NVA hit and stay with you until their casualties become unacceptable. I was moderately fluent in Vietnamese but never did pick up what slang the NVA called Americans.

One of the unexpected delights of this newsletter are the resources of the readers. One reader has put me in touch with a documentary film maker familiar with PTSD. I shall have more on this in the next update!

Depending on the terrain, rice paddies, triple canopy jungle, hills, units in the field usually walk from one location to the next location in a single file. One person walking directly behind the next person in several yard intervals.

At the head of this column is an individual called the "point man".

He is the primary eyes and ears for detecting the NVA before the unit ran into trouble. If he does his job correctly, the unit survives. If his attention lapses and he fails to detect signs that the NVA are close at hand, people die. Because of the intensity, the point man is rotated every few hours.

But, the severe focus for being acute aware of what is in the trees above you, the contours in the ground around you and the sounds from behind you ... does not end when somebody else was walking "point". Nor does this extreme sensitivity to your immediate surroundings stop when you come home.

Earlier this month, I went to visit both a friend and a family member at Ft. Miley Intensive Care Unit. Unfortunately, he was on the third floor. Since I don't do elevators, I took the stairs up the maze of closed doors to the second floor. That is as far as I got.

I came back the next day, explained the situation to a doctor walking down the stairs and he walked me up the stairs to the bedside of my friend. I would not have been able to do so on my own.

In fact, when Daniel was born in 1975 at UC Hospital, I had to wait two days for his Godfather to bring him down to the first floor before I ever touched him.

This is part of the day-in and day-out PTSD stuff you live with... and it gets old. For me. For my family and friends.

More of the slang used in Vietnam.

ASH AND TRASH: Helicopter term for flights that are considered non-combative (doesn't mean you aren't going to get shot at) such as taking men from the field to rear base camp, taking hot food out to the field, bringing supplies, etc.

A SHAU VALLEY: the A Shau Valley was one of the principal entry points to South Vietnam of the Ho Chi Minh Trail. The most famous battle of the A Shau Valley is known as Hamburger Hill.

BASE CAMP: a semi permanent field headquarters for a infantry unit usually within a certain tactical areas area of responsibility. Base camps contain all or part of a combat unit's support elements such as medical, supply or food service functions.

BEEHIVE: an artillery round fired directly into large masses of exposed enemy troops. Repeat use of this last-ditch weapon sends swarms of steel darts that simply pulverize human bone, muscle and flesh into unrecognizable mounds. Used as a primary base defense against ground attack. Very effective. Unforgettable.

BERM, LINE: A small built-up area of dirt which divides rice paddies; also, a rise in the ground such as dikes or a dirt parapet around fortifications.

BODY BAGS: plastic bags used for retrieval of bodies or body parts on the battlefield.

BOHICA: short for "Bend Over, Here It Comes Again." Usually describing another undesirable assignment. On any given assignment, somebody may die. On a Bohica mission, it is a guarantee.

BOOKOO: Vietnamese/French term for "many," or "lots of..."

BOONDOCKS, BOONIES, BRUSH, BUSH: expressions for the jungle, or any remote area away from a base camp or city; sometimes used to refer to any area in Vietnam.

BREAK SQUELCH: to send a "click-hiss" signal on a radio by depressing the push-to-talk button without speaking, used by troops in combat when speaking into the microphone would reveal your position.

BRING SMOKE: to unleash intense and extreme amounts of artillery fire or air force munitions on an enemy position.

Now to lighten the mood...here is the Army's definition of a cow:

A cow is a completely automated milk-manufacturing machine. It's encased in untanned leather and mounted on four vertical moveable supports, one on each corner. The front end contains: the cutting and grinding mechanism, as well as, light sensors, air inlet and exhaust, bumper and a fog horn.

Secretary of Defense William Cohen spent three days in Saigon/Hanoi in preparation for a Presidential visit by President Clinton later this year. Intellectually, I understand this. Emotionally, it is devastating to realize that the President of the United States is going to shake the hands of the same people who gathered old men, mothers and children as hostages in front of my command and then began executing them. I still hear their screams.

Sometimes it is several times a month. Occasionally it is hourly. The meds dull the senses but they don't stop the memories. This is when I curl up in bed and pull the pillow over my head. One, among many memories, that won't go away.

Questions and Answers:

Q. Since you started this project, have your feelings about the Vietnamese changed?

A. This is a minefield for me. Keeping the "should-have, could-have, would-have" politics out and concentrating on people deeply affected by Vietnam. And what has happened in them and their families since their return.

I am not proud to admit that I don't like crowds of young men running towards me ... regardless of their ethnicity. But I especially don't like large groups of young Asian men running towards me ...as in getting off a bus and running to catch the next bus. And the facts of history aside, there are South Vietnamese and North Vietnamese. And I don't like the North Vietnamese.

Can't say that I am overly fond of the South Vietnamese.

In spite of the above paragraph, I do not harbor intense feelings of hatred for the North or South Vietnamese people. Vietnam is an exceedingly poor agricultural based country where surviving from one monsoon season to the next is not a given. The 45 years of French colonization and Japanese occupation during WWII didn't help economically. But I do hate the NVA and their political leaders.

So I avoid situations where there are Vietnamese. As in employers, friends, medical workers, neighbors, Winchester (Los Angeles) and Santa Clara county. I don't what I would do if a family member or close friend became involved with one. And I definitely don't want them (family/friends) to feel the way I do about Vietnam.

A couple of years ago, when I was contemplating suicide, the ONLY thing that kept me going was that if I did, then the North Vietnamese won.

The NVA beat the South Vietnamese. But they didn't beat me.

Since I no longer pray, I can't find it in myself to forgive the NVA for some of the things I personally saw or heard them do to both South Vietnamese civilians and to Americans who strayed away from "safe havens". Somebody else will have to do it for me.

Words of wisdom learned the hard way:

When you have plenty of ammo, the NVA are not to be found. When you are low on ammo, the NVA are everywhere.

Corollary to words of wisdom...

Some days, your trigger finger gets just plain tired.

Sere

PS: The following comment is from a reader: "People have as much trouble talking about Vietnam and the Vet's experience, your experience, as the Vet's have all these years in talking about it. I think keeping us updated on your progress, steps you have to take, have taken is helpful....interesting.....encouraging. Information on the Vietnam experience that you also have in the newsletter is good, important, but probably difficult for people to respond to."

It takes a whole village to raise a child and ... it takes a whole community to heal a combat vet with PTSD.

Chapter 5

The events in Vietnam did not happen in a political vacuum in the United States and the world stage. The purpose of the following time line is not to teach but to gain a historical perspective.

Perhaps you may remember where you (or your relatives/friends) were and what you (they) were doing as these events took place.

1964

January 8: Lyndon Johnson calls for War on Poverty and greater efforts on civil rights in his first State of the Union Address.

February 2: U.S. Ranger VI lands on the Moon.

July 2: Johnson signs Civil Rights Act of 1964.

July 18: Riots break out in urban ghettoes of New York City and Rochester, the first of the series of African-American riots.

August 2: Johnson orders immediate retaliation for the attack on U.S.destroyers Maddox and Turner Joy in the Gulf of Tonkin, allegedly by the North Vietnamese.

August 7: Congress approves Gulf of Tonkin Resolution giving the President power to take "all necessary measures to repel any armed attack against the forces of the United States, and to prevent further aggression."

September 27: Warren Commission report is released.

October 15: Khrushchev is ousted, replaced by Brezhnev and Kosygin.

October 16: China detonates its first atomic bomb.

November 3: Lyndon B. Johnson elected President.

1965

March 8: Vietnam: First U.S. Marines in Vietnam wade ashore at Da Nang.

May 2: Johnson sends troops to the Dominican Republic to "prevent another Communist state in this hemisphere."

November: Battle of the Ia Drang Valley, the first major clash between the United States and North Vietnamese Army.

December 24: Vietnam: U.S. forces number 184,300 in Vietnam.

1966

January: ICBM, Minuteman II, with improved accuracy, enters service.

February: Vietnam: Senate hearings on the Vietnam War chaired by Senator Fulbright begin.

March 16: 10,000 Buddhists march in Saigon protesting U.S. support for corrupt Ky regime.

March 25: Anti-Vietnam War rallies staged in seven United States and European cities.

April 30: Chinese Cultural Revolution begins with Chou En-lai's call for anti-bourgeois struggle.

June 2: Surveyor I makes perfect soft landing on moon.

December: Vietnam: U.S. forces number 362,000 in Vietnam.

Maps play a very important part in the hour-to-hour life in the bush. Maps tell you where you are. It suggests the most likely places for NVA base camps, trails and ambush locations. If interpreted correctly, maps keep you alive by pin-pointing exactly where you want artillery fires on NVA fortifications or where a "Dust off" can make a pickup.

As a infantry officer leading troops in combat, I am responsible for knowing ACCURATELY at all times what our location is. To be sure, my second in command, also knows. But the responsibility is mine.

Unfortunately, I have yet to rid myself as of this date of having to know exactly where I am...at all times...even now. This obsession limits the places that I feel comfortable in going to ... such as weddings in South Lake Tahoe, funerals in Sonoma, trips to Yosemite, laser light shows at Knott's Berry Farm and much, much more.

And on those occasions, when I do venture out into Nature, I still find myself "scanning" closely for anything that appears out-of-place. I still look for likely ambush locations, where water is most likely to be found, if I had to go up that hill "what would be the best approach?", if I had to defend that potential helicopter landing site "where would I put my machine guns?". This mindset did not lend itself to good times for me on any of the family/friend camping trips in the 1970s.

And, even though I thoroughly enjoyed my Boy Scout activities in growing up, I absolutely hated it when Robert and Daniel went on their Boy Scout camping trips. All I could think of...was them lying hurt somewhere out in the woods.

It took me from 1969 to 1989 to explain to anybody who would listen just how much I hated camping.

In defining Posttraumatic Stress Disorder (PTSD) as according to the VA, some of the features of combat related PTSD are:

You have nightmares or "flashbacks" of traumatic combat experiences
Your sleep patterns have changed since Vietnam
Images of traumatic combat experiences pop into your mind
You avoid situations that remind you of Vietnam
You are tense, on guard, or easily startled by loud and unexpected noises
You feel like you cannot tell people about what happened in Vietnam
You become overly angry, irritable, or blow up at minor things in everyday life

Addressing the use of the word "stress" as defined in the workplace for me. It has always bothered me when supervisors make a point to let you know the daily stress they encountered. Rather than say anything, I kept my feelings about their stress levels to myself while inwardly telling myself they don't have a clue about what real stress is.

Was this attitude unfair to supervisors- Yes! In my mind, this "stressed-out" individual can always go get a drink of water, go home after 8 hours, take a shower, wear clean and dry clothes and reasonably expect 6 to 8 hours of uninterrupted sleep at night. Every night. And if the work situation really causes problems, this individual can always quit. In Vietnam, these options do not exist.

This attitude causes significant problems in my not allowing anyone to tell or suggest what they would like for me to do. And I am not real big on telling or suggesting to other people (in any capacity) what should be doing.

Monday through Friday, when I look out my window and see people in their cars or riding the bus to work, I get very jealous because I would like to enjoy some of the social benefits of the workplace. Gossip. Friendships. Shared histories.

More of the slang used in Vietnam.

C-4: a very stable plastic explosive carried by infantry soldiers. "C-4"is a plastic explosive popular among soldiers in Vietnam because of its various properties. It is easy to carry because of its lightweight, stable nature, and had a potent explosive power. C-4 would not explode without use of detonation devices, even when dropped, beaten, shot or burned. It was not destabilized by water, an important consideration given the Vietnam climate. Because it can be safely burned, "C-4"is popular with GIs, who break off a small piece of it for heating water or C-rations. Sometimes used in foxholes to warm hands and feet on chilly nights.

CLAYMORE: Widely used in Vietnam, the claymore antipersonnel mine is designed to produce a directionalized, fan shaped pattern of fragments. The claymore used a curved block of C-4 explosive, shaped to blow all its force outward in a semicircular pattern. A large number of pellets were embedded in the face of the explosive, creating a devastating blast of fragments similar to the effect of an oversized shotgun.

With their directional pattern, claymores are well-suited as a perimeter-defense weapon. With electronic firing, defenders in bunkers could set claymores in a pattern to cover all approaches and fire them at will. One problem with this is the tendency of the NVA to use infiltrators to sneak into the defense perimeter before an attack and simply turn the claymores around. Then, when defenders fire the mine, its fragments pepper their own position.

CONTACT: The condition of being in contact with the enemy, a firefight, also "in the shit."

There was humor in Vietnam. One particular incident, that I still laugh about even to this day, occurred when my platoon got the job of tracking down and eliminating a sniper that was upsetting some "REMF". This particular setting was some Nipa palm trees with moderate vegetation. Needless to say, playing "cat-and-mouse" with someone who knows where you are and you don't know where he is...can be stressful.

After several hours of this, one of my riflemen stands straight up and empties a 18 round magazine into the top of the tree right in front of him. The sniper comes tumbling down.

Since their snipers usually operate in pairs and sometimes threesomes, extreme caution is necessary. About 30 seconds after the sniper hit the ground, this monkey coming tearing down the tree at the rifleman and ultimately ends up biting him on the foot.

Needless to say, a "dust-off" is called in as my medic does not carry rabies vaccine. I still think it is funny. And so did the troops who witnessed it.

Another incident, that wasn't quite so funny, also involved snipers. After determining a sniper was in the rafters in a "hooch" (bamboo hut), I got covering fire as I made my way to its doorway. Placing my AK-47 down, I reach down into my ammo case and pull out a concussion grenade. Tossing it just inside the door that was inches away, I turn away from the door and place my fingers in my ears to dampen the concussion.

The next thing I know bamboo is flying everywhere. Instead of a concussion grenade, I used a fragmentation grenade and it had gone off about three feet from where I had tossed it. I was extremely lucky in standing upright when that grenade went off. The only damage done was that it took a while for my hearing to come back. What was even worse was one of the squad leaders coming up to me later and saying, in effect, if you are going to get killed by a hand grenade, next time make it a NVA grenade.

Several years ago, when I was first diagnosed with combat PTSD, my doctor suggested that I get out of the house and become more social. At one point, I was invited to a small and intimate dinner party where everybody knew each other very well from camping trips, picnics, kids in Scouting and church activities. At this particular time, I was heavily dosed with Xanax and other drugs and so I could barely walk or talk coherently. But the company was congenial and I sat in one place throughout the evening and thoroughly enjoyed the company.

During the course of dinner, one of the participants asked me to do a mathematical quiz. I declined as I was having a hard enough time staying awake and was politely listening to the conversations flow back and forth. This person persisted in my answering the quiz in that it was simple and would only take a second.

All eyes were on me as the dinner table grew very quiet as I struggled to come up with the correct answer on the first try. I distinctly and clearly remember my eyes filling up with tears and my cheeks burning as I ultimately answered the question. The problem is that everybody knows that I am having difficulties in walking and concentration. And, to be in the spotlight like this, is an indignity to me that serves no good purpose.

This quiz may have seemed simple to others. But it was hideously complex to me. There is a definite stigma to having PTSD. But severe mental illness does not automatically mean severe mental stupidity.

This event still rankles me two years later. And, to date, the individual involved still has no idea that serious bodily injury was about to occur.

Research shows anger management is a very hot topic with combat PTSD and that violent reactions linger just below the surface toward real and imagined insults or threats to personal safety. I think it is fair to say that most people do not react well to this kind of stimuli but PTSD people generally have a hair trigger response that can go from polite civility to rage faster than you can blink your eye.

Some people in VA discussion groups that I have attended are very well armed on their person and in their home to handle situations like this. Others- like me- do not keep weapons at all for fear of irrational acts. We know where to get them but figure that the delay provides a "cooling-off period" for sanity to prevail.

Does this mean that families and friends have to dance around discussing sensitive topics with PTSD people- No!! But it does mean that deliberate insults/threats or physical aggression can trigger immediate and serious bodily harm, if not death, to the offender.

Q & A
Last Sunday (April 30th) was the 25th anniversary of the fall of Saigon. How is that affecting you?

I do feel for the 600,000 Vietnamese that made their way via extreme hardships into refugee camps and were lucky enough to come to the US. The 1,000,000 or so "boat people" need to have their story told. The estimated 65,000 South Vietnamese starved and shot in "NVA re-education camps" makes me angry. Those who were exiled by force from their homeland and family is the gist of another documentary which I will leave to somebody else.

As far as the NVA is concerned. My polite answer is "Screw 'em" and that includes all their dead, wounded and PTSD people.

What has been the biggest disappointment in the documentary to date?

Getting qualified veterans willing to talk about their day-to-day experiences in Vietnam and current day-to-day circumstances on camera. Leads come in and then for one reason or another, they don't pan out. This is the point that I am in right now as I keep trying different approaches. A special update will be sent when I am successful.

Words of wisdom learned the hard way:

Whenever you drop your backpack to engage in a sudden fire-fight, your ammo and grenades will always fall the farthest away, and your canteen will always land at your feet.

Sere

PS: Some of the feedback that I am getting from the readers inquire if I am getting "better". The answer is "yes" but I can't "quantify" just exactly how. Somehow, I feel a little optimistic that, with broad exposure of this documentary, our PTSD experiences will not have been in vain and, maybe future generations of Americans policymakers and voters, will somehow avoid the mistakes of the Vietnam generation.

Chapter 6

To give you a more complete outline of what I am doing now, the following items have to be completed before distribution starts. I now have two combat vets with PTSD willing to interviewed on camera.

When we were out in the boonies, getting mail boosted morale and was eagerly looked forward to. A "Dear John" letter is the highest prize and is read literally by everybody in the area. Mail comes out via helicopter when an ammo run, replacement drop-off or tactical briefing is necessary.

On this particular occasion, a door-gunner (from a chopper) unexpectedly dropped off a batch of letters from a 4th grade school class from somewhere in Texas. Each letter was addressed "To an American Soldier somewhere in Vietnam" and was written by individual pupils. We probably got about 100 or so letters enough for everybody to get 3 or 4 apiece.

Because of the heat, we took a break and started reading the letters after establishing local security. Upon opening the letters, typically the students told us their name, how many brothers and sisters they had, how old they were, who their teacher was, and so forth.

Little did I know these letters would prove a tactical mistake on my part. Because most of the letters included artwork of soldiers, snakes, drawings of the Sun, bullets, helicopters and more.

And questions like: Have you killed anybody? Do you eat rice every day? My brother says killing isn't very nice. Will you visit our school when you return home? All written in the block letter penmanship of a 4th grader.

It didn't take long for the tears to flow from emotionally exhausted and physically sapped old men in young bodies. Young people whom we didn't know and would never meet ...cared about us. To a man, we all cried. Including me.

These letters did something the NVA couldn't do: render us combat ineffective.

For about 15 minutes, we were not paying attention to the NVA in our area. Our thoughts were elsewhere.

One of the hardest things I ever did in my life was to gather up all these letters into a pile and watch the flames turn this tangible link to our home ... redden and smolder into ashes before we moved out into an ambush position for the night.

Looking back on my return from Vietnam, one of the first inklings that I KNEW something was wrong took place as Robert, Stephanie and I were watching a Peter, Paul and Mary concert on TV. I had seen them live in concert at University of San Francisco and enjoyed their style of music very much. As the program neared its end, Peter Paul and Mary started to sing "Puff, the

Magic Dragon" as Robert sat mesmerized with his imagination soaring (he was about two years old).

To me, Puff is no longer the ballad of my college days. Puff is a C-47 (the type of aircraft used in the Berlin Airdrop) retrofitted with six Gatling machine guns that fire perpendicular to the fuselage and puts two bullets in every square foot of a football field in less than three seconds.

Puff lingers over a suspicious area, drop flares (at night) to illuminate the area and pulverizes anything above ground that indicates enemy activity.

As Robert sang along with Peter, Paul and Mary, it bought back memories of my using Puff to protect my men from superior NVA forces with more firepower than we had.

Stress is watching, on a moonless night, a blazing duel between five or six NVA machine guns with green and white tracers arcing into the sky, trying to hit Puff. And watching and listening to the same time Puff returning fire at these muzzle flashes on the ground. Just a half mile away from our night defensive position.

Then having the radio crackle with the mission of taking my 24 men to now go out and secure the downed Puff and any survivors knowing full well, that with that many machine guns in the area, there are a lot of NVA waiting for us.

Without a doubt, those men in my unit that survived Vietnam did so; including me, in part because of Puff. I still get a smile when I think of Puff. But the songs of Peter Paul and Mary no longer interest me.

Out in the boonies, extraneous talking is discouraged. Accomplishing the mission and bringing everybody home intact is the task. For me, the silent commentary goes like this:

"SHIIIIIIIIT"

"Did that bush just move? I thought so"

"Doc, Doc, Doc, How many times do I have to tell you, it is a knife wound. K-N-I-F-E. Not shrapnel. Of course, it hurts. Maybe you would like one. And just how am I supposed to keep the dressing clean and dry, you dumb shit?"

"Jesus, look how long that snake is. Now where did that sucker go?"

"Missed me, you bastard. Now make a noise or move so I can see you"

"Hold on Son! Dustoff is on its way. They are 10 minutes ETA. Hold on. You are gonna make it!!! Don't go into shock on me. Can you hear the chopper- We are popping smoke now. Hold on, you son-of-a-bitch, you are going home to Momma. You gonna make it!"

"Looks like we are surrounded. Again."

"OH SHIT, OH! SHIT, OH SHIT!! that hurts. What happened to my legs. Fuck!!!!"

"Does anybody at home care?"

"Damn you, Tybeck, why didn't you tape your grenade handles like you were supposed to. Now you are dead and you took Coleman with you. Damn you. Damn you!"

"So this is what it is feels like to die."

"Oh, God, please let me make to that tree line. Please! Please. Please! I want to have a family before I go. Shit, God, you really had me scared back there. Thanks, I can make it from here."

"I'm alive. My back hurts. My head is gonna explode. Wish I could see"

Where the above fits in... is that when I came back, I didn't talk unless it was necessary. I didn't have much of interest to say for 21 years. Not that anybody would have listened. And when I finally did say something to my best friend (whom I didn't see or talk to for three years after my return). He went nuts for four days. Not going to work. Calling me up and crying on the phone.

To this day, engaging in social chit chat is not something that I do easily. And I truly envy those people who can make the latest weather pattern, sports teams and newspaper headlines seem important.

I talk only when I have something to say to Stephanie, Robert, Daniel, Denise, Dyoni. And listening intently is more important than talking because others may have observed something that I need to know to bring us home.

And this established peculiarity is not fair to me. Or to my family and friends.

Words of wisdom:

When reviewing the radio frequencies that you just wrote down on your forearm, the most important ones is always illegible just when you need it most.

Signed:

Sere

PS: What is Memorial Day to you?

There are just too many memories such as a grievously wounded 21 year old field medic who's freshly arrived in the boonies and both you and he know that he's going to die before a "dust-off" can arrive. You're sitting there and talking to him and holding his hand and looking into and pouring water on his face and you can see his life force just ebb away and you know damn well, he just wants his mother there and you're the only parental figure that he's got, his life is just slipping away - and - there is nothing else you can do for him. So you pull out a pocket Bible and read the Lord's Prayer to him.

Then it dawns upon you that he has been with you for just four days and his body will be home before his first letters get there.

And you know that your life will never be ordinary again.

There is nothing more intimate than sharing someone's dying with them. This medic should have had a chance to grow up and had grandkids, he should have had the chance to die in bed of old age with his family gathered around him.

Each of the Army's 30,905 battle deaths, the Navy's 1,626 battle deaths, the Marine Corp's 13,082 battle deaths, the Air Force's 1,739 battle deaths and the Coast Guard's 5 battle deaths [total: 47,357] was somebody special to a Mother, Father, brother, sister, aunt, uncle, friend, neighbor, spouse or child.

For those engraved into the Vietnam Memorial Wall, you have to wonder just what they would say to us- Memorial Day isn't just the last Monday in May; because, some months have several Memorial Days.

P.P.S.: It is very difficult to put down these vignettes of Vietnam service. But I do it for the purpose of inviting conversations that should have taken place 30 years ago among family and friends among all who read the updates and watch the documentary. Even if you don't know what to say, just acknowledging them is important to me.

Last week, I received the following comment from the adult daughter of a Vietnam Veteran who is reluctant in sharing his Vietnam experiences.

"Thank you from the bottom of my heart for the detailed, thought-provoking, and informative email about "Coasties" in Vietnam. I truly had no idea until now what my father and hundreds of other men like him were asked to do while patrolling the coasts during Vietnam.

All of my life I've wondered what my Dad was REALLY doing over there - what - he might have seen, heard, and done....Although he does not feel comfortable disclosing any of this information to anyone in our family, I now have a much better sense of this part of his history. I hope that he and I can have a dialogue about his experiences if and when the time comes - and if he ever feels compelled to talk about it."

I absolutely treasure comments like this.

Chapter 7

Testimony was presented before the U. S. House of Representatives Committee on Veterans Affairs that estimates 296,842 disabled seriously mentally ill veterans use the Veterans Administration mental health service in a given year. Some have PTSD. Some do not. These patients have disorders which are complex, disabling and chronic in nature. And these disabilities adversely affect all aspects of basic life functioning.

At the moment, the following four combat vets will talk about some of their experiences and what has happened to them since Vietnam on camera. As you watch and listen to their narratives it is helpful to remember that they are special to a wife, child, mother, father, uncle, aunt, friend and neighbor.

Bill
Wellbutrin seems to work. Special Forces medic. Bad motorcycle accident was trigger in 1994. Instinct bow shooter. 100%. Wife was 22 when she married him at age 40. Doesn't tell war stories but does describe his feelings. Writes and read poetry as stress reducer. Saw my brochure on toilet wall at VA. He is now 57 with an 8 year old son.

Was on a Channel 4 documentary around 1982 as a patient in Menlo Park. Finnish and Scottish ancestry. Was in Vietnam for 7 months. Part of the Cambodian invasion force. Got married in 1988. Has worked odd jobs such as painting, boat wright and fisherman. MOS was 05B40 on a B team. Communications specialty. Was in the Tay Ninh area.

Pepper
173rd Airborne Brigade from 1967 to 1969. Was a 11Bravo and 11Charlie. Lives in a community house. Saw my brochure at Ft. Miley in Building 8. Finally went home to New Orleans after 31 years.

James
Piano technician. LRRP. Drafted and not trained for LRRP. Works out of his house down in Moss Beach. Best time to reach him is days. Major surgery at Ft. Miley. Understaffed caused problems. Bronze Star.

Joe
Called me on June 8th. A friend of his called to ask if he would be eligible. Then Joe called me. We set up a 7:00 am June 10th telephone interview. He was a door gunner. Still drinking. Door gunner in 1966 to 1967. With 17th AHC in the Mekong Delta. Drafted and sent to Ft. Ord from Pittsburgh, CA. Trained in helicopter school at Hunter Army Airfield in Georgia. 100% PTSD. Came back and was angry at the draft dodgers. Very patriotic when he went over there. Has had a lot of jobs including NAS in Alameda. Been in and out of jails for 15 out of the last 21 years. In one year, he will be through with his parole obligation. His wife is Asian and has cancer. Has a daughter 3 years old and grandkids that are 5 to 7 years old. 55 years old. Born on July 15th 1945. Major problem with drugs upon return. Been in and out of Menlo Park.

It appears to be somewhat easy to make a bad documentary in terms of inadequate sound, poor lighting, bad camera angles and the like so I am in the process of jumping through Channel 26 hoops by using their facilities and interns/volunteers to professionally light, floor manage, audio and record the interviews better than I would be able to on my Sony TRV-310.

Recently, I was asked "I have a question for you. I know very little about life in the military, especially during combat, other than what I have learned from you. My question is: How long were you (or a typical ground trooper) out on patrol or whatever it is called before you got a break of some kind? Where you were relieved from the front lines and could go back to some sort of camp where you could sleep in a cot & get a shower, for example?"

In my unit, we would be away from our firebases (think of forts in the cowboy movies as an analogy) typically 10 days to three weeks at a time.

On a firebase, a company of infantry (80 to 100 men or so) would be stationed there for maybe two or three days before they would go back out in the boonies and another company would come in a perform local security. This cycle would repeat itself on an irregular basis among the four infantry companies that would be assigned to a firebase.

When a company is on a firebase, they are subject to mortars, sappers, sniper fire, machine gun and ground attacks. But hot food is available, the luxury of unending amounts of ice cold water is *highly* appreciated by all. Showers consist of a canvas bag hung from two poles and when you press down on a nozzle and the water sprays down on you. Invariably, the water is warm from the Sun. When a shower is completed, a fresh set of battle clothing is given to you as the old set would be dirty and ripped.

If a boonie soldier needs dental or other medical attention - gum disease, foot fungus and/or fevers of unknown origin. At some point they would go back to a major Base Camp. Think Presidio of San Francisco in size.

At this location, everybody has access to cots to sleep in, sheets, hot water for showers, movie theaters, barber shops, telephone service back to the states by ham wave operators (who donated their time) and probably most amenities found in any small town. But it is not a free ride for those stationed in these areas as they, too, are subject to intermittent mortars, rockets, and ground attacks. Over 85% of the soldiers in Vietnam lived in these base camps and provided services to those who operate out of the aforementioned fire bases. The other 15% lived and worked their entire tour in and around the firebases.

1967
January 27: Outer Space Treaty limits military uses of space, signed by the United States, U.S.S.R. and 60 other nations.
February 14: Treaty of Tlatelolco, signed in Mexico by all Latin American states except Cuba, prohibits the introduction or manufacture of nuclear weapons.
June 5: Six-Day, Arab-Israeli War begins.
June 17: China explodes its first hydrogen bomb.
October 18: Soviet Venus IV probe lands on Venus.

December: Vietnam: U.S. forces number 485,000 in Vietnam.

1968
January: Prague Spring reforms led by Alexander Dubcek in Czechoslovakia to bring about "socialism with a human face."
North Korea seizes U.S.S. Pueblo with 82 members aboard.
January 30: Tet Offensive, attacks on South Vietnamese cities by North Vietnamese and NLF troops.
March: Vietnam: 77 day siege of Marines Khe Sanh(Vietnam) ends.
March 16: My Lai massacre in Vietnam.
March 31: Johnson withdraws from U.S. Presidential race.
April 4: Martin Luther King, Jr. assassinated.
June 5: Robert F. Kennedy assassinated.
July 1: Nuclear Arms Nonproliferation Treaty signed by the United States, U.S.S.R. and 58 other nations.
August 20: Soviet invasion of Czechoslovakia ends Dubcek experiment.
October 31: Johnson halts bombing of North Vietnam, invites South Vietnam and the Viet Cong to Paris peace talks.
November 5: Nixon elected president.
December: Vietnam: U.S. forces number 535,000 in Vietnam.

1969
March: United States bombing of Cambodia begins.
June 8: Nixon Doctrine and " Vietnamization " begins. Nixon orders first troops out of Vietnam. U.S. forces number 475,200.
July 20: Neil Armstrong and Edwin Aldrin land on the Moon.
September 1: Muammar Khadaffi comes to power after coup in Libya.
September 3: Ho Chi Minh, Communist leader of North Vietnam, dies.
November 15: March on Washington draws record 250,000 anti-war protesters.
November 17: Strategic Arms Limitation Talks (SALT) begin between the United States and U.S.S.R. Limitation Talks (SALT) begin between the United States and U.S.S.R.

The reason that I include slang is that this is the way your father, husband, brother, uncle, nephew or friend talked in the boonies. Discussions about stateside politics including anti-and pro-war demonstrations, movies, television, sports and other non-Vietnam issues is almost non-existent. The vast majority (in my opinion) just want to do their job and resume their lives as soon as possible. The slang that I mentioned is both the day-to-day vocabulary and mind-set.

DET CORD: An 'instantaneous fuse' of a long and thin flexible tube loaded with explosive. Used to trigger the simultaneous explosion of multiple Claymores in ambush. Additionally used to fell trees by wrapping 3 turns per foot of tree diameter and detonating to make room for helicopter landing sites in dense jungle.

DUSTOFF: a nickname for a medical evacuation helicopter or mission. "I need a Dustoff" became the call as boonie troopers got on the radio for a mission to pick up wounded soldiers in the field ...often under fire. When a soldier is hit, the call goes out for a Dustoff, and any

26

helicopter in the area, without a higher priority mission, can respond. This didn't necessarily mean that there is a trained medic aboard. Some Dustoff missions do have a medic. Most did not.

Flying Dustoffs takes enormous courage on the part of the crew as ground fire from NVA is the rule ...and not the exception. The reward is that wounded soldiers get to medical facilities in 10 to 15 minutes, and for serious wounds, each minute of flight becomes critical for survival. In addition to the wounded, Dustoff also take out the dead. Sometimes in body bags, occasionally wrapped in a blanket. And, more frequently, just the body.

"How-to-Do-A-Tracheotomy-With-One-Hand-and-Fly/Shoot-With-The-Other' became routine for the 21 year old pilots and door gunners flying these missions.

Dustoff crews come and get you even if your intestines are literally hanging down to your feet, at night, in the rain, and surrounded by NVA.

In 1969 - Dustoffs flew 120,841 missions and evacuated 241,151 patients. 37 crewmen were killed, 138 were wounded and 61 helicopters were lost to enemy action. I am one of these missions ...groggy in-and-out of consciousness and watching helplessly as bullet holes zip through both sides of the fuselage and the M-60 door gunner returning fire at the NVA on the ground.

It seems that the more people (63) on this list, the less feedback I get. In June, I got a total of two responses including a comment from a reader who saw the traveling Vietnam Wall exhibit in San Carlos. It helped her get in touch with the strong feelings that many of the Vietnam casualties aren't on the Wall.

I am beginning to wonder if this documentary is a just a feel-good project with no lasting impact coming forth. For the 58,000 dead. Or the 400,000+ living dead.

Maybe the truth is that the vast majority of Americans didn't care about our day-to-day experiences then. And they don't particularly care about our day-to-day experiences now.

Definitions of fear learned the hard way:
Fear is watching 2 Phantom Jets speed forward of your position just above treetop level and knowing that they had already released their napalm canisters BEFORE they were directly overhead of you.

Another way of making your heart jump and thump is to pump a couple of rounds into a advancing NVA who is firing directly at you and watch his body impact from your shots as he still keeps coming at you. From 50 feet away. So you go from firing one round every time you squeeze the trigger to full automatic and literally cut his body in half before he is in your face.

And this is not the sort of thing you feel comfortable in telling your kids, wife, family or friends. Even 50 years later. But it is the reality for an invisible minority of Vietnam veterans. Whose stories will go the grave without being heard. Because no one really wants to listen.

Chapter 8

Several weeks ago, Stephanie and I were returning home from my first workshop. It was about 9:00 PM. Almost, but not quite dark. As we turned a corner, I spotted four people standing over someone, fully clothed, laying face down on the sidewalk. Not knowing if this was a situation of street violence or a medical emergency of some sort, I found myself bounding out of the car toward the individual down on the ground. As I got closer, I saw that these were "gangbangers" with their bulky jackets and pants falling over their butts.

Pressing my finger against the side of his neck to check for a pulse, I found myself automatically checking to see if his breathing was deep and regular. And finding that it was, I started asking questions (interrogated ...looking back) as I turned him over looking for signs of violence. Not seeing any, I gently started slapping his face and propping him upright. He came to and then told me what had happened.

It seems that he and his buddies were driving down the freeway and a truck threw up a rock that had almost completely shattered the windshield in front of him (he was riding shotgun) and that subsequently, he had gotten himself so worked up emotionally that he had hyperventilated. His friends carried him to the car and they sat there for a few minutes before they took off. Stephanie had called the police from the car by this time with the details that everything seemed alright.

We went home and I went to bed almost immediately. I tossed and turned and stared at the ceiling until 3:00 A.M. It dawned upon me that each of the participants were Asian. The whole episode from the time I jumped out of the car until I returned was probably five minutes.

Fortunately, I had my once-a-month meeting with my psychiatrist the next morning at 11:30 and we discussed this incident.

I was not fine with the fact that the "combat" mindset from 49 years ago had automatically kicked in. I do remember thinking as I approached the victim that if these four did have knives or guns, I have been in this position before, and that several of them would die before I did.

This mind set is NOT the way to live. And I am more than tired of it. More than tired.

More of the slang:

DI DI MAU: move quickly. Also shortened to just "Di Di."

D.I.E.: draft-induced enlistment. This was the Army's term for guys who "volunteered" only because they were about to be drafted.

DINKY DAU: Vietnamese term for "crazy" or "You're crazy."

DUFFLEBAG: the oblong, unwieldy bag in which troops stored all their gear. Also, an artillery term for motion/sound/seismic sensors placed along suspected enemy trails or areas. Dufflebag sensors contained small radio transmitters which sent a signal to an intelligence unit when triggered. Once triggered, the artillery fired on the "dufflebag" target to intercept or interdict the NVA.

FAC: forward air controller. A light plane pilot who directs air strikes and artillery fire from the air.

FIGMO: acronym for "Fuck it I got my orders." As in "figmo chart," a shortimer's calendar with numbered sections which are filled in, one each day, as the shorttimer keeps track of days to go for the Freedom Bird.

Freedom Bird: the jet aircraft which flies returning servicemen to the U.S.

Grunt: an infantryman,

Gunship: armed helicopter with the primary mission of fire support to grunts in actual contact. Hanoi Hannah: the Tokyo Rose of the Vietnam war.

Ho Chi Minh sandals: sandals made from old truck tires. Worn by the local populace as well as the NVA. South Vietnamese forces generally wore the same jungle boot that US forces wore. Some specialized US units wore jungle boots with ripple soles that imitated the Ho Chi Minh sandal footprints.

Ho Chi Minh trail: the complex of jungle paths through Laos and Cambodia which served as the principle Viet Cong and NVA supply route.

After being medi-evac(ed) to a hospital, I came to as I was being given an IV and strapped down on a stretcher. Somebody had taken my glasses and put them in my shirt pocket. It didn't matter as I couldn't see very well anyway. As I dozed in-and-out of consciousness, at some point I found that I had been moved outside a tent that was providing welcoming shade from direct sunlight.

Overcome with the moans and groans, prayers, screaming going on around me, I looked around as best as I could, I saw that strapped down on the stretcher next to mine was an NVA officer was a nasty head wound. I could see the grey matter that was his brain from where I was inches away. He was moaning Mother over and over. I made a fuss at the South Vietnamese guard watching the prisoners. As best as I could in my limited Vietnamese, I asked the guard to release me from the straps at my chest and legs pinning me down in the stretcher. He asked me "Why-"

"Because I am going to kill this son-of-a-bitch"

And the guard just laughed at me.

Just one hard judo chop to his nose area is all I wanted. I would have killed the bastard. In front of the doctors, nurses, other wounded and anybody else in the area. I am sorry that I didn't get a chance. Even though it has been 31 years.

When I am up at Ft. Miley, occasionally I strike up a conversation with veterans from WWII and Korea and I make it a point to ask them how they feel about the Germans and Japanese today based on their war experiences.

In general, the answers are a mixture of hatred and forgiveness.

I have the hatred. You can do the forgiveness.

When You Cross Paths With A Lonely Veteran, Ask Them:

"Do You Feel You Have No One To Talk To?"

"Do You Feel All Alone In Meeting Your Daily Challenges?"

"Have You Recently Lost Anybody Important In Your Life?"

And if you feel like you want to help improve the quality of life for a lonely, visit https://companions.lpages.co/many-veterans-have-no-friends/ **to see how you can help …**

Chapter 9

The Channel 8 Telethon that happened several weekends ago was absolutely terrific for me! Since everybody involved wore several "hats", I got to be a "live" camera operator showing the hosts, do data entry into the computer for keeping track of the amount of money raised. In addition, I had the chance to do some of the grunt work of setting up the studio with the backdrop cloths, setting up tables for product shots and much, much more!

I worked 6:00 to 11:15 on the Friday. Took Saturday off. Came back Sunday from 2:00 to 11:45 pm. And was emotionally exhausted until Wednesday. Since then, I have taken another workshop on audio production ...use of a "mixer" for blending audio coming from a cd player simultaneously with host and/or guest talking. Tedious to the max. A talk show might have 24 separate microphones coming through the mixer at any one time as the program is broadcast.

With any luck, I am hoping to begin taping my studio interviews within the next several months.

An ice-cold glass of water is a welcome treat. Water that is clean tasting. Water that is purified. Water that is abundantly available. Water that smells fresh. And water that you can see through.

Turn on the faucet and it comes bubbling out ...cascading over the glass while wetting your hands and occasionally splashing your face. And probably taken for granted by most people in the US.

One of the harshest situations in the boonies is water. To drink. And to keep clean. EVERYBODY carries at least two plastic

canteens (quart size capacity). Some carry four. The red dirt and dust, combined with the heat, causes great soreness. The nose becomes dry and feverish. The "grit" gets between your teeth, and your eyes became blurry from the sweat dripping down from the 3 pound steel helmet you are wearing. Dirt finds its way into your eyes, mouth, ears, and hair. Jungle boots gradually fill with dirt that penetrates clothes and ground in at the neck, wrists, and ankles, and when mixed with the daily perspiration, feels like sandpaper on raw skin.

If not involved in a firefight, in very hot weather a break would come during the hottest part of the day. The traditional Vietnamese siesta time is 12:00 to 2:30. This is the usual resupply time for replacements, ammo, food (sometimes a hot meal which includes ice cream and 2 cans of warm soda each).

Enough time to loosen your shoelaces and empty shoes and attend to calls of personal hygiene with whatever water is available. Thirst always wins over cleanliness.

On some of these occasions, a "bladder bag" is carried underneath the resupply helicopter. Think of a greatly oversized bean bag with nozzles every 18 inches around the circumference.

Frequently ...it is ice-cold. Which prompts immediate headaches among those of us with parched throats. Since this was combat, the chopper does not stay as it attracts unwanted attention with its blades (and noise) spewing up dust columns for all to see and hear.

Resupply helicopters come out every three to four days. You make do with whatever field expedient water or food sources are available. It is a given that the river, canal and stream water are contaminated with generations of animal and human waste. Typhoid, cholera, dysentery and water-borne illness of every type is on your mind each time you drink from these canals. As if you have a choice. The NVA do not have resupply helicopters and therefore drank wherever they can.

If fresh water isn't available, alternatives are irrigation canals with raw sewage, bomb craters and the morning dew on the plants. Going into a village to use their well (if they have one) is absolutely the last option as word of your presence would be hastily passed along to whatever NVA are in the area.

For those of us operating in a stealth mode ...this is hazardous to your health.

Americans die doing stupid things to slake their thirst. Perhaps the next time you look at a frosty glass of cold water on a extremely hot day ...think of us.

If the dust and the bake-your-head temperature is not enough to annoy ...then mud, cold, rain, and wind during the rainy season effectively take their place. Rain becomes the greatest discomfort a boonie trooper could have. At least, when it is hot and night approaches ...it cools off. When it rains, it is day and night.

Wet clothes, boots, and poncho liners(blankets); wet feet and wet ground; wet small arms and equipment; wet ground to sleep on, mud to wade through, swollen rice paddies to cross, and other discomforts came with rain. There is no comfort on a rainy day or night except under your poncho liner. Cold winds blowing rain in your faces increases discomfort. In the rainy season, you never get or stay completely dry. Mildew sets in. Jungle rot turns your feet and toe nails yellow.

Mud often surprises you as to its depth, and at times, it is necessary for one man (or more) to pull another to hard ground. With all concerned breathing and sweating profusely and voracious cussing of every religious, civilian and military authority one could think of.

Night patrols during the rainy season have additional hazards (besides the NVA) such as falling off bamboo bridges spanning the irrigation canals, stumbling into ditches, ripping your face open or slipping and sliding and poking your eyes into bushes, tree stumps and fallen branches.

Rain or not, we give precious sips of water from our canteens to wounded NVA.

And 49 years later, I still hate being wet. If I could shower and shave without getting wet, I would.

Ft. Miley is like home to me. While waiting for appointments, I sit in the waiting area watching television and reading magazines and participate in fleeting or in-depth conversations with other veterans. I have yet to run into anybody that I knew while I was on active duty.

For now, this is my social activity since movies, clubs, libraries and shopping malls are not an option. The vast majority of the veterans I come into contact with do not have PTSD but are dealing with all manner of medical situations. Some very serious. Some trivial.

But there is one part of Ft. Miley that I avoid. It is the pharmacy. And I am irresistibly drawn to it every time I am on the grounds.

The waiting area in the pharmacy consists of 22 chairs facing four prescription dispensing stations. Take a number and wait your turn. That part does not bother me.

Bringing me to tears is watching the parade of men my age with baseball caps and embroidered names of Vietnam or US Army 1966 or USMC 1969 in oversized jackets and the shriveled skin of old men. Some in wheel chairs. Or speaking so softly that you cannot hear them because their hands are cupped over their mouths or clasped over their heads. Just like me. They are me. I am them.

There is no privacy and you can easily overhear conversations between the pharmacist and the veteran. Occasionally, a very elderly parent or adult child and sometimes a grandchild (as young as 10) chaperons the vet to talk to the pharmacist because the veteran has PTSD and unable to comprehend what meds he is getting, when to take them and/or when the prescription needs refill. Much less what it is for. And I get tears everytime I see it.

Because I think back to my young men sweating profusely, gasping for breath and covered in their own vomit who were so full of life ...in struggling through endless firefights and dustoffs. In the heat. In the rain.

For this ... 49 years later-

Several weeks ago, Robert and I were in Vacaville and had some extra time on our hands waiting for morning traffic to ease for a return trip back to San Francisco. We decided to take in the sights and sounds of Travis Air Force Base and its Air Force Museum.

In August 1997, when I had my second meltdown and was partially hospitalized at Ft. Miley, I underwent a series of EMDR sessions. One of which required me to write about an episode in Vietnam that troubles me.

" ... After the battle was over, I told my platoon sergeant that I was going home on emergency leave and would be back in 30 days. I reported into the new doctor that had arrived with the medic-evacs earlier and told him I was leaving for a medical emergency at home. As I did that I nearly fainted. The next thing I knew I was sitting in the door of a "dust-off" with other wounded with my pack on and the AK-47 still in my hands. I lapsed into and out of consciousness as the crew chief strapped me to the webbing so I would not fall out. I remember him asking for my AK-47 and I said no.

The next thing that I remember vividly to this day was being on a stretcher and a nurse slapping the shit out of my face as she said "We're losing him!" as they carried me into a first aid tent. I remember thinking I am going to shoot you. I was stripped down, given a number of shots and IV while the corpsmen pulled shrapnel out of my legs. While this was going on, I had a death grip on the AK-47.

Apparently, they gave me something to sleep and I woke up on a cot with a medic standing nearby who said as soon as I was ready I would be going home on the next medic evac flight back to Travis Air Base in California. My AK-47 was gone.

My flight home was aboard one of the giant C-141 Starlifter cargo planes that had been adapted for carrying wounded soldiers. There are doctors and nurses aboard who tend to our needs as we make our way home. I ask one of the orderlies if I can be of help. He says yes and I am taken to the side of a LLRP (long range reconnaissance patrol) soldier who is very badly burned front and back, top and bottom, side to side and in-and-out. His flesh is pulling away from the bandages.

The orderly asks if I could use the ice and water beside his stretcher to keep his forehead and lips wet with moisture. Almost the entire rest of his body was is in bandages. I don' know his name and he is delirious as he floats in and out of consciousness from the various painkillers.

Somewhere in the flight, he gets some clarity and asks where he is.

I hold his left hand and tell him he is on a medic evac home and that I will hold his hand until we land at Travis. I ask him what is his name and where does he come from. He mumbles something which I can't understand. I continue to talk to him and hold his hand continuously throughout the 16 hour flight home as the doctors and nurses keep changing his bandages at regular intervals.

As the plane touches down at Travis Air Force base and is taxing over to the waiting line of ambulances, I lean over and whisper to him that he is home. He dies as his hand relaxes out of my hand and falls towards the floor.

His war is over. Mine continues to this day.

All of us gave some part of our lives. Some of us gave all of our life. He did.

EVERY time I think of those who are bored by my (our) Vietnam experiences, I get absolutely enraged. There is room enough for all shades of opinion on the Vietnam experience. I thought so when I was in Vietnam. I think so now. For those weary of our stories, tell me "Where the hell were you?"

Sere

Lesson learned the hard way: Discovering that jagged pieces of white-hot shrapnel burning into your flesh hurts beyond reason ...and that monster waves of pain will knock you silly as medics use probes and pliers to pull it out. If you survive.

Chapter 10

Most readers of the updates do not have military experience. With that in mind, the following is a reference point for previous/future updates.

I am a platoon leader. There are three rifle platoons and one weapons platoon in a U.S. infantry company. A battalion consists of 4 or more infantry companies. Medics are in short supply with 3 or 4 medics per company.

My primary job as a 23 year old platoon leader is to take my platoon and close in with the NVA by means of effective firepower (read: bullets hitting people) and maneuvering in order to kill, capture or destroy them or to repel his assault by fire, close combat, and counterattack. 24 hours a day. Seven days a week.

My secondary job is to take care of my people. In other words, in military parlance, performing the mission comes first. Keeping casualties to a minimum is subordinate to accomplishing the mission.

In theory, platoons are organized into three rifle squads of 10 men each plus a weapons squad of 9 men and a platoon HQ of a lieutenant and two men. The men are equipped with M16 rifles and M79 grenade launchers. In reality, a squad is between 5 and 10 men led by a sergeant.

Weapon squads contained M60 machine guns and 90 mm recoilless rifles for busting up bunkers.

In theory, a platoon had 45 men on the roster. In Vietnam, the platoon in the field is about 25 men. Under strength platoons make up under strength companies to form under strength battalions. Wastage is high in all units due to rotation, illness, injury, wounds, death, Relaxation and Recreation leave, etc. As a result, infantry companies are always short handed in the field.

In addition, we have stealth missions where our job varies from grabbing an NVA/VC officer or tax collector, (often called "Snatch Missions"); tracking NVA companies and platoons as they come across the Cambodian border by following 200 yards or so behind them until ARVN or US forces could effectively meet and greet them; getting to downed chopper/crews before the NVA do and much much more.

These missions put a premium on mastery of fear. Fear of the unknown is the soldier's biggest worry. The unknown takes many forms. A new area where you haven't operated been before, a new enemy unit or a new friendly unit working beside you.

Of necessity, these missions require us to infiltrate into an area without being seen or heard. Each a volunteer with advanced expertise in infantry skills (land navigation, camouflage, marksmanship proficiency with rifle and machine gun, escape and evasion, hand-to-hand combat and so forth).

Naturally, the NVA do the same to us.

This leads to innumerable chance encounters and deliberate full scale clashes between squads, platoons and companies on both sides as US & ARVN troops dance with NVA/Viet Cong forces. Survival depends on your ability to out think, out move, and out fight the NVA in close combat.

A little humor that says a lot. Upon encountering a Cobra in combat, different types of units react differently. Some examples:

* Civilian: Runs away from the cobra screaming.

* Paratrooper: Kills the cobra.

* Armor: runs over cobra, giggles, and looks for more cobras.

* Army Aviation: Uses the Global Positioning System for cobra's location. Still can't find cobra. Goes back to base for crew rest and 5:00 PM drinks at the Officer's Club

* Ranger: Assaults the cobra's home and secures it for use by friendly cobras.

* Military Intelligence: analyzes all available intelligence and national asset input on the reptilian situation; reports sighting of Godzilla to National Command Authority in Washington DC

* Navy SEAL: Expends all ammunition, several grenades and calls for naval gunfire in a failed attempt to kill the cobra. The cobra bites the SEAL, then retreats to safety.

* Artillery: Kills cobra, but in the process kills several hundred civilians with a massive Time on Target artillery barrage with three Field Artillery brigades in support. Mission is considered a success and all participants are awarded Silver Stars.

* Marine Recon: Follows the cobra and gets lost.

* Forward Observer: Guides the cobra elsewhere.

* Green Beret: Makes contact with the cobra, builds rapport, wins its heart and mind, then trains it to kill other cobras.

Eight years after my return from Vietnam, my Mother died unexpectedly. For a period of time prior to my leaving, alcohol played a major role in her life as she drank herself into oblivion several nights a week. By the time she died, much to her credit, she cleaned up her act. We did not get along because I wanted to be the best infantry officer that had ever been. Didn't date extensively. Drove a ratty old car. Spent time exhaustively studying Army field manuals in detail. And soaking up combat knowledge from Korean and Vietnam veterans like a sponge.

When I was in Vietnam, I never wrote my Mother. Just didn't have anything to say. As a matter of fact, I forgot what she, my Dad, my sisters and my brother looked like. When

I got a letter from Stephanie, it took my some time to remember that I had a fiancé. Much less what she looked like.

From the vantage point of years, I now wonder what my experience was like for her- As a military wife, did she "jump" everytime the phone rang- Did she look out the window at the cars in front of the house before she answered a knock at the door- Did she stop reading the newspaper after learning that the US was losing 1,200 people a week when I was there-

When I came home, I never talked to her about my experiences in Vietnam. Of course, I didn't talk to anybody else about them either. My Dad had been in WWII and Korea but it was 26 years before we ever had a serious discussion about my Vietnam activities. I just didn't have anything to say.

Writing these updates is turning out to be like peeling away the layers of an onion as different experiences bubble up from the past. My Mother is better off for not knowing them.

I wonder what she would think if she saw me now.

You are at 1,200 feet altitude. It is 3:30 AM. A half moon illuminates the earth below. 34 of you are crammed into a C-119 over an area definitely hostile to American uniforms. So none of you are wearing one.

Alternating currents of cold chills and fires of rage pulsate up and down your back as payback time approaches.

The red light comes on. Three minutes to drop zone. "Outboard leg stand up! Sound off for equipment check!". Snaplinks are attached to the static line. Series of jump commands follows as each trooper double checks his neighbor's equipment for perhaps the 187th time.

Yellow light flashes. "Lock and load all weapons!" One minute to drop zone. "Stand in the Door!".

Green light blinks "GO!" and two sticks of 17 people each shuffle out of the door as fast as they can. Both hands clasped tightly around the reserve 'chute on your belly. Knees together. Toes pointed straight down. Reassuring jolt as static line blossoms your chute.

Two minutes later, you are on the ground. The C-119 drones away in the distance.

You are alone. And expendable to accomplishing your mission.

It is spine tingling quiet as you hastily gather your black T-4 parachutes and quickly bury them and check for injuries/lost equipment before you clandestinely move out to your objective a mile away.

A one word coded message goes over a "secure channel" to the C-119 notifying that you are in position and that everything is OK.

Authentication/verification comes quickly your message is received by the chair-borne commandos at Yankee Station {the Internet will tell you all you want to know} and subsequently patched into the bowels of the Pentagon. From now on, your radio frequency is monitored in real time 12,000 miles away.

Your next transmission comes if you are detected or just before you initiate hostilities at the objective.

Overhead and out of sight and sound, several fighter aircraft on MIGCAP establish local air superiority. Phantom and 'Thud' strike aircraft are in route with the latest air-to-ground munitions should heavy concentrations of hostile personnel or armored vehicles make an unexpected appearance.

The nearest friendly force is a SEAL team (also monitoring your frequency) some miles away that has prepared for your possible extraction under fire. You explicitly remind all concerned that being taken prisoner is not an option. You will see to it for them. They will see to it for you. Everybody knows what to do.

And so you go into combat formation and move across the rice paddies to your objective. With nobody feeling particularly ten feet tall and bulletproof. If successful, in due time ....your mission will be on the front page of major newspapers across the world.

Decent men. Extraordinary circumstances. Some die before the morning sun comes up.

And some 49 years later, when you talk with other veterans ...this experience and others like it ... are not available for conversation.

And so it colors what you say to other combat vets as well as your family and friends.

As days and years flow by ... bit by bit ... the world of people comfortable with you shrinks as they go about their lives. Sincere invitations for "get-togethers", quiet evenings, or whatever slowly evaporate to nothing. Until your life is spent alone in a bedroom. With a computer.

With the exception of four individuals, even the e-mail you get comes only after you badger with three or more personalized messages over several months. But you get plenty of "FW's" of friendship and jokes from the same people who don't respond to your e-mail.

And so you think "Is this the best I have to look forward to?"

You are emotionally spent. And you have known that for 49 years. I would guess that most people grudgingly get out of bed in the morning. For some of us with PTSD, the reaction that I hear and share is "Aw, Shit! I am alive" before they get out of bed. If they get out of bed.

And it dawns upon you that all you had to do was to stand up when you were crawling on all fours or walk out into an open field, sneeze while listening to NVA relax among themselves or any number of other things. If you knew then what you know now, you wouldn't be here.

But you are. Damn it.

Dying was easy. Staying alive is the hard part.

From time to time, your opinion is sought on current military activities. And you quickly turn the conversation into what they think about the current military activity. Because, in truth, almost to a person ...they are much more interested in what they are going to say than in what I might have to offer.

Thank you, America ...

For conversations with medics sprinkled over the years with the words "Electro Shock", "Concussion(s) ", "Delusional", "Shrunken Hypothalamus", "PTSD", "Agent Orange", "Chronic Dislocated Shoulders", "Anti-Psychotics", "Unemployable" and "Brain Chemistry Imbalance".

For not knowing at age 23 that the best years of my life are over ...

For all the jobs I got fired from within 2 to 4 weeks after being hired ...

For being able to identify the human heart, lungs, liver, kidneys without benefit of medical school. For sticking my hands deep into a open chest and massaging a faltering heart back into a regular rhythm. Even though I just shot him a few minutes earlier ...

For friends and family members reminding me that it is OK to smile ...

For my inability to watch people eat meat ...

For needing a psychiatrist at age 24 and not getting one until I was 44 ...

For my inability to make new friends without having to tell them why I have not been in the work force for the past 4 years ...

For not being able to play baseball/basketball with Robert and Daniel like other parents as they were growing up because of my shoulders ...

For friendships and relatives lost based on my Vietnam experiences ...

For confusion, disorientation and babbling in front of Stephanie, Robert and Daniel. And for being too embarrassed to talk on the phone ...

For the non-NVA Vietnamese that may have bought delight and joy into my life as friends, co-workers and neighbors.

For not teaching ANYTHING in detail about WWII, Korea or Vietnam in high school or college for future generations to learn from.

From every cell, tissue and organ in my body, thank you very much ... politicians, voters and non-voters of America.

Based upon the 9 previous updates, if YOU received the following from individuals who were draft deferred or too old for the Vietnam experience ... how would YOU respond---

"...I do not believe it's good for you to tell and in some cases repeat your story. Each time I hear your story it (to me) seems that you become more depressed. I believe it is time for you to leave your story behind and move on."

"... you and your 5 veterans are still living in the past. If you still need to tell your story, my question would be "how long do you need to keep telling your story-"

Sere

Lessons learned the hard way: Watching a Mother and her infant children stranded in a crossfire hurts. Especially after she goes after a child that panics and runs out into the open. Dragging the children away from the Mother after she dies ... lingers forever.

Some days you take prisoners. Some days you don't.

This is one of them.

Chapter 11

"The Wall That Heals", a half-scale replica of the Vietnam Veterans Memorial Wall, will be on the grounds of Ft. Miley from November 9th to November 16th. For those who won't/can't talk to me ...go and talk to them. The names listed have all the time in the world.

Each of the Army's 30,905 battle deaths, the Navy's 1,626 battle deaths, the Marine Corp's 13,082 battle deaths, the Air Force's 1,739 battle deaths and the Coast Guard's 5 battle deaths [total: 47,357] is somebody special to a Mother, Father, brother, sister, aunt, uncle, friend, neighbor, spouse or child.

I*n the jungle ...daylight is always subdued and filled with shadows*. Night comes instantly with the dim light of day replaced by blackness so dark that you cannot see your fingers at arms length.

Flashlights with strong red filters are the only way of reading maps for bringing in air strikes.

And with the darkness comes the normal jungle noises from unseen animals, birds, insects. whatever.

Darkness has the illusion of movement as brushes, trees and vines move. Eyes strain. Ears strain. Hours pass as centuries as you struggle to stay awake. Taking a leak down your pants leg as you lay in the dark is the norm. Waiting. Waiting.

It is true that when the noises of night creature in front of your position suddenly and totally stop, someone or something is out there that has not been there before. That means get ready to rock-n-roll. Right now!!!

Operating in NVA territory and remaining undetected means using natural cover and concealment of bamboo tree groves, rice paddies, small hills, irrigation canals and jungle vegetation. As much as possible moving during darkness or the early morning mist to take up locations during the day to cover likely avenues of NVA approach.

In infiltrating an NVA base camp and taking out a sentry, absolute silence is critical before-and-after as there is no second chance.

I am more than amused by war movies showing the bare hand over the mouth and the upward stab. Experience shows he will bite a chunk out of your hand and you will yell. Loudly. Then you have to catch him before he hits the ground. Other techniques involving nooses are much quieter. And efficient.

I use to live for Sundays to watch football. It's fun to watch 22 grown men push/pull/throw a ball 100 yards. Grunts. Groans. And all that.

But several weeks ago, I was watching and then suddenly I got sick to my stomach. Running to the bathroom, it occurs to me what is wrong. It is surprising that I didn't pick up on it before.

It is the umpires.

Throughout the game, the umpire perform certain hand-and-arm signals to indicate transgressions of the rules.

In the boonies, I give hand-and-arm signals to indicate actions to be taken. Even when not directly engaged in combat, one man can only yell so loud. And with people spread in combat formation, everybody cannot hear you so ... so you use arm-and-hand signals to indicate what you want done.

For instance, using one hand to tap the top of your helmet is "Cease Fire". With rifle in hand, extending both arms over your head indicates to a chopper pilot that you have picked a spot for him to land. Circling one hand rapidly over your head and then extending two fingers and pointing in a specific direction indicates "Silent killing, two men. That direction. Go!"

Knowing the NVA has similar hand-and-arm signals identifies that person as a leader to be quickly killed or silenced. Even though I am watching a football game, when I see the umpires signaling ... a chill comes over me. I know that it has been 49 years but somethings still stand out in the mind.

In absolute fairness, this revelation came slowly. I knew that football occasionally spooked me but I didn't know why. Now I do.

I haven't watched a game since August.

Part of the shit you live with.

Within the next week, I will make a formal presentation to management at Channel 8 for a twice monthly series on Vietnam Veterans. Several of the staff have tentatively agreed to help with the details of getting the program up and running.

Still more of the slang ...

DEROS: date eligible for return from overseas; the date a person's tour in Vietnam was estimated to end.

DOC: what grunts call medics.

ELEPHANT GRASS: tall, sharp-edged grass found in the highlands of Vietnam.

EXTRACTION: voluntary or involuntary withdrawal by air of troops from any operational area via helicopter.

FAC: Forward air controller.

The forward air controller (FAC) has the responsibility for calling in air strikes on enemy positions Usually flying a low-level, low-speed aircraft, such as a single-engine Cessna, the FAC identifies VC/NVA positions and relays the information to attack aircraft, helicopter gun ships, or high-altitude bombers.

At Ft. Miley, six of us met weekly to form friendships, share job/housing/transportation/food information, compare experiences and strengthen ourselves and each other that tomorrow will be better than today. Occasionally it is. Mostly it is not.

We have each lost part of our tribe or rather our tribe has lost us or at least isn't willing to find us in spite of our weird sense of humor, oversized stomachs, scruffy beards and clothing twenty years old. We are alone.

Several weeks ago, Someone that I hold near and dear made arrangements for us to go to an air show full of vintage airplanes, acrobatics single seaters with a flyby of the Blue Angels. Since I don't get out much except for a weekly visit to Ft. Miley and a internet class at Skyline College, I thought this is a nice change of pace.

Arriving at our vantage point on the top of a parking garage four stories up, Someone backs his truck into a parking space next to the four foot high concrete ledge separating us from the 40 foot drop to the pavement.

Since we have several hours before the bi-planes begin their acrobatics, we window shop and I buy Stephanie a present. Upon returning to the truck, we notice two little boys sitting on the lowered tailgate. One is about four, the other is about seven. They are there with their Dad.

Striking up a conversation with him, Somebody and I welcome them to enjoy the show where they were ... so they didn't have to move. And so we bring out the lawn chairs and blankets and sit back waiting for the festivities to begin.

At some point, the Dad decides the four year old needs a better vantage point and takes him off the tailgate and places him directly on top of the ledge. Without holding him. Since I am getting my Sony camcorder ready at the time, I don't notice.

Within the space of 10 feet of the child are probably 15 adults.

When I finally look up, I glance at Someone and say "I can't deal with this. I need to go back in the truck". So I do. With the windows up. And my hands over my ears so I don't hear the child scream when he falls.

A child screaming in terror is one of my PTSD "triggers" that causes me instant rage.

Since I had already taken my regular dose of meds for the morning ...the extras that I had bought along would take a while to kick in. So I try to distract myself by saying "I am an adult. Surely, I

44

can tell the Dad that his behavior is making me extremely uncomfortable and that they both were welcome to sit back in the truck with us."

And then, I think what if he says "No. Mind your own business".

What do I do?

Call the police? They could take forever to get here.

And then I decide "If the child falls, I will kill him".

My hands shake as I pull Stephanie's emergency card of what I am to do in public places when I get disorientated and cannot think logically. It says "I will find the nearest security personnel and show them my VA card, explain the situation and ask for help".

I am reading the words but they aren't registering. The lights are on but there is no one home.

Ft. Miley is seven miles and thirty minutes away.

I am having a panic attack. Despite my best efforts. Full fledged.

My eyes go blurry. And my breathing deep and erratic. Headache pounds me.

And the only thing running through my mind is that I am going to ask him to remove that child from that ledge right now. If he doesn't, I will kill him on the spot for endangering that child.

I touch the door handle to get out of the truck, Someone knocks on rear window of the truck and says that the Dad has now put the child back into the bed of the truck.

It takes me an eternity to calm down. The ability to think logically eventually comes back.

Probably most normal people react in some manner when they see a child in danger. But I am not normal. And I know that. In life-threatening situations, military people do not sit around pondering about what to do next.

I got enraged at an air show. Last year, it's the first day of my Basic Film Class at Skyline College when I tell a Vietnamese youth that wants to sit next to me at the only empty seat in the classroom that it would be hazardous to his health to sit there.

Nine years ago, it's a supervisor at UPS who makes the mistake of waving an American flag in my face and ... before I think ... I have him up against the wall with every intent of seriously hurting him. This is not the way to live.

What's next? Thank you, America.

While I do not speak for any other combat related PTSD individuals, I think that I can safely say that we value other people's lives to the extreme. Especially children. Our lives have been forfeited. But NOBODY has the right of parenthood to physically endanger a child in our presence. And expect to live.

When I get home that evening, nine month old Hailey decides she wants a "Grandpa & Grandma " fix and comes over for the evening. So I lay down on the bed and cradle her like I cradled others who would never see their parents in this lifetime again ...and gently rock her to sleep.

And, after she is asleep, I cry myself to sleep. Wishing I never wake up.

I have heard/touched/seen too many dead children. And I don't want to listen to another die. Ever. For those inclined to give me a spiritual sermon ... don't bother. I don't want to hear it.

The Someone driving the truck is my oldest son ...Robert.

He watched/listened to his Dad publicly lose control of his emotions.

Again.

It is OK to have emotions. It is not OK to lose control of them. In front of your children or anybody else.

I am beyond tired. Tiredness that saps joy from watching Hailey smile. Or Stephanie laugh. Are you listening, God- You weren't there at the concentration camps of Auschwitz-Birkenau in WWII. Nor were you present in the rape barracks in Kosovo. Why should I expect you here now?

Some of us are hurting pretty bad down here. In case you hadn't noticed.

It is time for us to return home. We have done our tour.

Sere

Founder
Things that flash in your mind when riding in the car, walking along the beach with a relative, browsing in a neat bookstore with a close friend, reading e-mail, putting infants to sleep, slurping breakfast or watching television.

When shot, people drop like a brick in a swimming pool, bow from the waist and sit down or cartwheel into bushes, tree or canals. Arms, legs and heads literally fly off the body when hit by machine gun fire. Some clutch their chest/stomach area. And this doesn't include sounds.

One of the most sickening ...is made when you drag a wounded man and listen/feel his body twitch as he is hit a second time. And again. And again ...when the others around you ...throw up on you ...when you reach shelter.

Hope you are not bored.

Some are.

Somehow they won't quite make it to the Wall in San Francisco.

Hope you do.

Chapter 12

"Hi Sere -

A few notes to say hello and to wish you all the best this Christmas Season. I have been following your progress via the newsletters and I read them thoroughly. I am sorry that I haven't contacted you this past year to discuss them.

You know how it is with paying rent, keeping the cars running, keeping an eye on my parents as they age older and keeping up the kids has me hopping so I am sorry that I haven't made the time to keep our friendship a two-way street. I guess a real friend is the one who walks in when the rest of the world ignores you or walks away. Looking back over several of the newsletters, I am struck by how much different paths our lives have taken. I am not sure that I could have done what you did. Sometimes when I read your updates, I have to stop and skip over certain parts because my stomach gets kinda of sick and I get depressed.

When I see "Vietnam Veteran" in the news, I think of you and other veterans that I know. Cousin Blake on my Father's side was in the service in WWII or was is Korea? He's always been a little quiet. Drinks a lot on occasion. But really is a nice guy. Come to think of it, he and his wife don't go out much except to family parties. Maybe I'll talk to him about his experiences in the Service. That is what you want, isn't it. Maybe it's difficult to talk with you but I can talk to him. Kinda funny in a perverted way.

There is a older Vietnamese lady at work. I see her in the coffee shop every now and I always say "Hello" to her. She seems nice but keeps to herself. Do you hate her too? Maybe someday, you two can talk. Well, maybe, judging by your updates that's not too good of an idea.

I guess that's why we haven't got together over the last several years. I'm afraid that I or someone else will say or do something that sets your "triggers" into motion. And I don't want to be responsible for that.

I don't know what to do. I'd like to remain friends with you but after reading some of the stories scares me about you and others like you. You seem to be such a gentle and caring person but I had no idea that such a violent streak within you remains active 49 years later. That is one of the parts about your newsletters that scares me. I don't want you mad at me.

I'm also having great difficulties in not judging what you did in Vietnam. Since I didn't walk in your shoes, I know this is wrong. But it is the way I feel.

Making the donation to help you with the documentary made me feel good. But I didn't realize there were strings attached. I wasn't prepared for that. To be honest, I really don't read them for sometimes months on end. And then I feel guilty because I know you put so much effort into them. But I know if I read all of it, I can get upset and I have enough other concerns in my life without adding yours. So I don't what to say to you.

From reading parts of the updates, I get the feeling that I never really knew you. Sometimes when I think of you, I am troubled that you don't practice religion any more to help you over these rough spots. I do anything I could to help you, I hope you know that. Some people like you silently come into our lives, leave footprints in our memories and we are never ever quite the same again.

The people in my life did not go to Vietnam like you did. I guess somebody somewhere took their place and that makes feel guilty when I hear "Vietnam Veteran". But you know, in a way, I am also a Vietnam Veteran.

"I was totally fucked up by some of your responses in your October edition e.g. "...I do not believe it's good for you to tell and in some cases repeat your story...etc...Who or what do they think they are if in fact this was their father, son or husband, I am willing to bet money their responses would be different."

Well, that's all for now. Please keep the newsletters coming. Can't wait for the documentary to come out. I really must go now. In spite of everything that has happened in your life, please excuse me when I say "Merry Christmas," and I'll think of you and your family on Christmas.

I think of you often and I'll write more often next year, I promise. If I could give you one gift this Christmas Season, Sere, I'd give you the gift to see yourself as others see you, so you could see how special you really are.

Regards,

XXXXXXX

PS: You've always sign your letters "Sere.......Founder. " What kind of organization is this- I am a little afraid to know the answer but I am asking anyway-

A little Vietnam slang. A little Vietnam humor from another writer (not me):

"One of the thing that always perplexed me when I was in Vietnam was the origin of term "C rations"- Are these rations the successor to "A" and "B" rations?

Of course we abbreviated everything so we just called them "C Rats" while the freeze dried long range patrol rations became "Long Rats"?

When we had guard duty at night, we had "One Man Up". If there were five of us for that bunker one could be up while the others slept and then, when it was your turn, your buddy would wake you and they could sleep. A less secure area might have "50% Up", translation, "not much sleep."

On this one occasion, I was on guard duty one night and things were pretty quiet for us in the bunker; but, not too quiet because of the Army outpost next to us. Their post had something to do with trucks and they tall wooden tower on top of which was an M60 machine gun. Their gun would usually be firing all night.

We never did understand what they were shooting at.

Suddenly, the one on rotating guard duty awakened us all. He heard something immediately in front of our position. We had no barbed wire in front of us but the hillside was mostly clear with some small shrubs and plants. This night we were blessed with bright moon light so visibility was very good. There are sounds that are natural and there are sounds that are made by man and this was not the sound of nature. We heard something immediately in front of our position and it sounded like a faint metal scraping sound.

But, we could see nothing- We called the duty officer for the night and he put the whole battalion on alert. It was decided that illumination was necessary so that we could see.

Pretty soon the whole hillside was lit up. Finally, my quest for the origin and meaning of terminology had been answered. Someone before us had eaten C Rations and tossed the empty cans out in front of our bunker. There were rats the size of small house cats scraping around in these cans trying to get out the last morsels of food.

This gave new meaning to the term "SEE RATS". "

Some time ago, I was asked if anybody wore/carried "lucky charms". At that particular moment, I couldn't remember. It has been a while. But then it came to me.

I did.

Literally, just before I got on the plane, Stephanie gave me a small crucifix even though our religions differ. I put it in my pocket and promptly forgot about it. Later, after I had been in-country for a while, I lost it when we were in ambush position for the night. Just before we were to break out of our night position, I discovered that I had lost it. Next thing I knew, there were 17 people including myself keeping our eyes pealed for the NVA that were looking for us and searching for the crucifix.

Somebody found it.

I never lost it again.

When I came home, I told Stephanie about it. Since we were about to get married. She took it to a jewelry store on Clement Street in San Francisco and asked the owner what could he do to make it into a wedding ring set. Somehow he did. And that is the wedding ring that she and I both have.

Only now, she wears hers.

Ultimately, the wedding ring didn't do me any favors. So I don't wear mine.

Sere

PS: Any other comments you care to add will be appreciated.

What I have written over the past year is part narrative and anecdotal information that shows we are real people like ... perhaps your father, son, brother, friend or neighbor. We are not all faceless unknowns on television news. Nor were we trigger-happy pot smoking baby killers.

Somewhere back in time, we were ordinary people caught up in a situation not of our making.

We are out of Vietnam.

Vietnam is not out of us.

Lesson learned: ***Decisions made by someone above you in the chain of command are seldom in your best interest.***

PPS:
Several have inquired about The following form letter is appropriate:

Past and current history shows, the species known as homo sapiens, is genetically incapable of making and conducting intelligent choices necessary to its survival.

As witnessed by genocides of the Armenians and Turks, the rape of Nanking, Native Americans in the 19th Century, the 60,000,000 people who died in WWII . Or the 32,000 children that die of starvation every day ...by United Nation's figures.

Humanity sucks. The sooner this failed experiment in evolution passes into oblivion, the better for other living creatures with morality/intelligence to flourish.

Thank you for your interest.

Chapter 13

You are 1 mile away from the Cambodian border. The NVA are now coming in from Cambodia in company and battalion size units(600+) during the daytime. There are 24 of you stalking a NVA company making no secret of their presence.

Your radio-telephone operator yells a flash immediate message that you have unknown size NVA unit with dogs on leashes moving rapidly in your direction. A passing helicopter just saw them.

From being the hunter, you are now the hunted.

No need to panic. You immediately send a radio signal to your Tactical Operations Center with the direction, size and rate of march of the NVA you are stalking.

Then you stop and immediately take advantage of nips and tucks in the ground around you ... and ... set up a hasty ambush for the unknown size unit coming your way. Since they can come from any direction, you form a circular ambush. All you have to do is wait.

And wait.

24 sets of trigger fingers cramp in anticipation of what is to come.

How many are there? Where are they?

Dogs?

Even though blazing heat from the Sun is baking your head like a furnace ...your entire body shivers.

Finally the dogs and their NVA scouts come into sight and sound.

You.

Switch to the radio frequency for the artillery unit supporting you and ...with well-practiced ease the following standard operating procedure dialogue ...begins

"This is Knight Six. Over! "

"Contact! Fire Mission! Over!"

This means that you are in actual contact with NVA or within seconds you will be exchanging fire. Somewhere, off in the distance, up to 24 individual pieces of artillery are alerted that you need help.

Right now!!!

"Unknown size NVA force closing in our location. Request marking round at map coordinates AN111111. Over!"

Those in pursuit of you are getting a "Time On Target" (TOT) fire mission. A TOT mission involves timing and firing of high explosive shells so they all hit on the same location at the same time. Some firing rounds that burst on the ground ...others burst in the air. The effect is that a particular location is quiet and peaceful one second; and, in the next second, it becomes totally enveloped and saturated with explosions in the air and on the ground. Typical kill radius is 30 yards for a 105mm and up to 80 yards for an 8 inch round.

Within a few seconds, you hear "Splash!" from the Fire Direction Center controlling the artillery supporting you. Splash means a shell is in the air and impact is seconds away. From this impact of this one round, you send corrections of distance from the shell's impact as to where you want it.

Total elapsed time approximately three minutes.

I bring you this technical information to illustrate several points. First the kill radius is 30 yards for a 105mm and up to 80 yards for an 8 inch round.

This means that if you are in open terrain and running or moving on all fours within the kill radius, you are virtually guaranteed to get hit with white-hot metal fragments. I say virtually because, depending upon the contours of the ground where the impact is, the fragments ricochet off trees and other solid objects and spray unpredictably.

Secondly, from personal experience, if you are lying flat on the ground within the kill radius, you can be lifted completely off the ground. Thus making you vulnerable to other artillery impacts and small arms fire.

Artillery explosions moves jagged white-hot metal fragments at 2000 feet per second and does terrible things to humans. A high explosive shell impact ...knocks fillings from teeth, pulverizes bone into mush, rips flesh into mounds and; on occasion, literally vaporizes the entire body ...except for the occasional foot or ear.

For those of us within the killing radius and protected from the shrapnel ... it gets worse.

The shock waves from the impact makes blood flows out of your mouths, eyes, ears, noses and asses. The headache knocks you to your knees. Everything, including body parts flying apart, moves in sloooow mooootiooooon. Pungent odor of high explosive Cyclonite empties your sinuses. Heart rate goes to 200 beats-per-second and accelerates from there. Ruptured eardrums create absolute silence. Insanity overwhelms all thought.

Been there. Felt this. Hated it.

What is important here is that your survival totally depends upon somebody else paying attention to detail under conditions of stress. Give the wrong map coordinates or the person on the other end reads them incorrectly ...and bad things happen.

A number of years ago, Carol Burnett starred in a made-for-TV movie as a Mother who was not given the correct information about how her son died in Vietnam. The movie chronicled her efforts to know the truth. And it was based on a true story about wrong map coordinates fed to the artillery. It was called Friendly Fire.

For me, this translates today into anger for those who do not check their "coordinates" before they make statements. Without providing some sort of reference point {third party verification}. For me, the map is my reference point. As an example, telling me what other readers think ... without actually knowing all the people and then conducting a poll ... upsets me.

I truly want to hear what your comments. Not what you think other readers think ...especially without even knowing who or even where they are. Readers of the updates vary from Hawaii to Alaska and Maryland to New Mexico. Much less California. Some are combat Vietnam Veterans. Includes Asians, Blacks and Whites. Half men. Half women.

This rigid attitude of ascertaining my facts carefully before speaking even in idle conversation is a carry-over from the Vietnam experience. And, for this habit, I apologize.

Before I went overseas, I enjoyed the easy give-and-take of casual conversation about topics of the day. Since returning, my conversations lack social "fluff" and are invariably serious in tone and content. I wish it was otherwise.

Even my babytalk with one year old Jazz has serious undertones. I am aware of it. Just don't know how to break it.

A sudden firefight ensues. A man goes down. Taking advantage of lulls in small arms fire going back and forth. You make your way over to him. His chest/stomach is a disaster but he has a chance. He fingers the goo that is his ribs and internal organs. Your medic is 150 feet away and pinned down in an irrigation canal by an automatic weapons fire. You care for him as best as you can while directing your troops with arm-and-hand signals.

The situation deteriorates rapidly as the NVA has far greater numbers and firepower on you. Your radio-telephone operator gets on the horn and requests emergency gun ship support from whomever is in the area.

You have bitten off more than you can chew.

Everybody hunkers down from the machine gun fire now sweeping your position. Through strict fire discipline, no one returns fire until he has a definite target. We do not have unlimited ammunition. It might be a while before we get more. So the age-old motto of "One shot. One kill" kicks into action.

Your senses come alive as the grove of Nipa palm trees around you fall apart. The branches come tumbling down from the .51 anti-aircraft machine guns the NVA are using against you. Congratulations! You are up against a NVA battalion as this weapon is not found in platoon and company size NVA units.

There are 24 of you.

The radio crackles that air support is on its way. "Puff" is ten minutes inbound your location. Artillery has yet to respond as other American units are also under attack.

You are on your own.

The machine guns start chopping down the tree you are hiding under. They are maybe 100 yards away. You have to move or die. The wounded man is now unconscious. He will surely die if you leave him. So you grab his belt with one hand and fire your AK-47 with the other hand ...directly at the machine guns as you move from your position and drag him with you.

Dust is everywhere. You feel the ground shake-and-dance from bullets impacting all around you. Everything is sloooooow motion. Vigorous covering fire from others in your unit allow you to drop into a nearby bomb crater with the wounded man.

NVA bugles and whistles signal they are maneuvering into position to overrun you. Everybody is holding their fire unless they have a definite kill. They can't kill you if they don't know where you are.

The welcome "Karuuumph" of a marking round of artillery becomes the most beautiful noise in the world.

Your radio-telephone operator is now the Man. He gives your location to the FAC now overhead.

The world around you explodes as volleys of artillery fire perform a 360 degree circle around your position. A walking barrage of firing between you and the NVA provides some protection while moving the impact point into the NVA. All you have to do is to wait it out.

And so you do.

Meanwhile, the wounded man lapses in-and-out of consciousness. He points to his chest pocket. You reach into the pocket and pull out several crumbled and faded pictures. He is smiling. His parents- And a crucifix.

He is dying. His vital signs are increasingly erratic. His moans go clear through your bones emerge.

You put the pictures into his hands while laying the crucifix on his forehead.

His eyes dart back-and-forth between you and your pistol. He points to your pistol. You know what he wants.

You are still on your hands-and-knees and gasping for breath after dragging him away from the trees. You risked your life for him and now he wants to die. Damn him!!!

Wine sipping, book-writing living-in-a-library theologians are many, many miles away.

So are his parents.

You are 24 years old and need to make a decision right now.

With pistol in hand and repeating the Lord's Prayer, you look into his eyes. Perhaps ..."What would YOU do under these circumstances-"

To this day you wonder ...what THIS North Vietnamese Army officer ... would do ... if the roles were reversed-

Another experience that bores those who explicitly state "...I do not believe it's good for you to tell and in some cases repeat your story. Each time I hear your story it (to me) seems that you become more depressed. I believe it is time for you to leave your story behind and move on." "... you and your 5 veterans are still living in the past. If you still need to tell your story, my question would be "how long do you need to keep telling your story-"

Fuck them.

Some experiences you never forget. Some attitudes you never forget.

This is one of them.

Signed:
Sere

P.S.
Lessons learned the hard way:

Never share a foxhole with anyone braver than yourself. Or put another way: Never draw fire; it tends to irritate everyone around you.

Chapter 14

Sounds ...

The "thud" of your shovel as you try to dig a few more inches deeper into hard red dirt for protection ...

The snores from your comrades blending in with the crickets ...

The clamor of a distant machine gun disturbing your half-sleep ...

The "hiss" of something you cannot see because ... everything on the ground is either black, brown, yellow or green ...

The mechanical sound of a round being chambered into a M-16 waking even the sleepy heads first thing in the morning ...

The "Whoop! Whoop! Whoop!" as the Dustoff above you lowers its jungle penetrator through the canopy to take out a heat stroke victim ...

The music of insects coming alive just as soon as the Sun goes below the horizon ...

The "baaaahh" of the water buffalo greeting you from 50 feet away as everybody points their weapons on full automatic at him ...and you walk gingerly around him in hopes of not provoking his charge at you. Hoping that nobody takes a shot at you at this very moment ...

The shout of "Jesus Christ" as a F(uck) U(you) lizard suddenly scampers across the top of the water in an irrigation canal momentarily unnerving everyone ...

The song "We've Got To Get Out of This Place" playing over and over in base camps from dozens of portable tape recorders ...

The stomach-churning "gurgle" from a man with a neck wound as he chokes to death right in front of you.

The steady "swish" of half-filled canteens moving towards you in the night ...

The "kkrummmpp" of a booby-trap exploding waist high forever ensuring the victim will never father any children ...

The "ooomph" as a bent over tree branch cracking into your ribs as you gingerly make your way up the trail

The "snap, hiss and pop" of your field radio tuning in the correct frequency for an air strike on those black pajamas coming up the hill at you ...

The white-hot "sizzle" from machine guns the NVA use to shoot down helicopters and fighter aircraft now dropping chunks of wood from the tree above you ...

The nightly clamor of mosquitoes circling your face as you sleep with a blanket over your head anytime you are near a bomb crater or flooded rice field ...

The cold mechanical "rat-tat-tat" of a body bag being zipped up ...

Sounds roaring like Niagara Falls ...

32 years later.

Last Saturday (January 27th) was the first taping of Vietnam Vet at Channel 8 (now called Channel 26). The nite before ...I couldn't get to sleep until about 4:00 AM. This is significant later. I got up at 8:00 and fed and played with Hailey until her parents came to pick her up later that morning.

Needless to say, I already had my introductory narration written out on 2' by 3' easel paper. Maps.
Mementoes. Photographs and more at the ready ...including a list of 74 typed questions to keep the conversations flowing freely.

I got to the TV station about 12:15 and worked with the other volunteers to arrange the set (jungle theme), position the lights appropriately and attend to the tedious details of seating arrangements, camera angles and audio checks.

There were two guests. One, a nurse, who joined the Army just out of college because she wanted to travel in the United States. The other ...a Marine.

Neither guest knew the other but were able to establish a bond that defies description even though each had totally different experiences in-country.

As it turns out, I never did refer to any of the 74 questions that I had prepared. We talked a little about what their life was like before they joined the military ... some of their experiences in Vietnam ... and reflection on how their lives had been impacted.

Moments of tears, laughter and silence.

The one hour taping ...went so fast ... that we were just getting started good in heart felt emotions that it was time to end.

And so it did. Every component fell into place. Smoothly. Easily. Effortlessly as the Channel 8 staff and volunteers made that extra effort to put forth a broadcast quality product suitable for "airing".

In fact, the taping went far smoother than I had any right to expect. And I had far more volunteers willing to help me get this program on the air ...than I had any right to expect!!!

The taping ran 1 minute and 28 seconds over our 58 minutes and 30 seconds of allotted time for a one hour show. Now, the Director and I have to edit and come up with a final version that will be ultimately broadcast to potentially 41,000 people in the Pacifica area.

The taping was finished at 3:40 PM. But the day wasn't over.

Because Channel 8 was having its annual Volunteer Thank You Dinner at 6:00 PM, I stayed to help set up for that event. Moving chairs and tables and that sort of thing.
During the course of the awards, I got a plaque that said "Volunteer of the Year". I was most surprised!

Most surprised!! And it is now sitting above my desk next to my cherished Elvira poster.

Soooooooooooo, it was a long day. After helping clean up from the Volunteer Party, I got home at 11:30 pm. Got to sleep around midnight. And didn't wake up until Noon on Sunday.

At which time, I got up for two hours and then went back to bed for some serious sleep.

For those who are normal, what is the big deal of being awake 16 hours straight-

Because ...it probably has been three or four years for me.

As important as the taping was, of far greater significance to me ...is that ...I have found a family at Channel 26.

Your Father is career US Army stationed in West Germany. President Kennedy and Premier Khrushchev make headlines daily in armed confrontations as Russian fighters shoot down Air Force surveillance planes off Norway. The US Navy imposes a naval blockade and boards Russian ships bound for Cuba looking for ballistic missiles. A U-2 spyplane is shot down over Cuba by a SAM [surface-to-air missile]. Bay of Pigs. Russian and American tanks face each other ...100 yards apart ... at Checkpoint Charlie at the Berlin Wall.

Every week or so, East German border guards machine-gun another family escaping to a better life in the West. Occasionally somebody survives the guns, mine fields, barbed wire and guard dogs. Europeans start hoarding food.

People in the United States listen to sermons about whether it is ethical to keep your neighbor out of your home bomb shelter. "Duck-and-cover" drills become routine in the nation's elementary and high schools. "Better Dead Than Red" are editorials. The movie "On The Beach" is two years old.

Every month, as a regular security measure, NATO forces go on "Alert" from Defense Condition Three to Defense Condition Two (also known as DEFCON). (DEFCON 1 is when shooting has started). Usually these alerts last from several hours to several days and then everybody returns to their regular garrison duty.

Tanks, infantry, helicopters and fighter aircraft as well as field artillery are in forward fighting positions ready to absorb an initial Soviet tank thrust into West Germany. You live 60 miles from the West Germany/East Germany border.

Emotional tension runs at fever pitch in Europe and particularly among the estimated 150,000 American dependents (wives and children of US soldiers) living in West Germany.

Because you are at "ground zero" for either conventional or nuclear war.

During the Berlin Crisis, one day your Father comes home early from work and says things are getting most intense. President Kennedy has decided, in a show of solidarity with NATO, that American dependents(of military personnel stationed in West Germany) will not be evacuated back to the United States.

He hands you a .45 standard issue Colt pistol. With ammunition. He says "If a Russian or East German comes through the front door, shoot him".

You are six minutes of Soviet bomber flight time from the border. Intermediate Range Ballistic Missile flight time is even less.

You are 16 years old. With a very frightened Mother and two younger sisters and a younger brother to protect.

You don't even know how to drive and you are the man of the house while your Father is away.

Sensing the tension and seeing the tanks, trucks and helicopters swarming about, your normally happy 3 old brother grows very quiet one day and asks you "Does it hurt to die?"
And you say "I hope not. But if it does, I will be right beside you all the way. So go outside and play and let me worry about it, OK!"

Some conversations you NEVER forget. This is one of them.

You hate Communists. And ...after talking with concentration camp survivors with their numbers tattooed on their forearms ...you aren't all that thrilled with Germans either. Especially after visiting Belsen-Belsen on a high school field trip.

Seven years later, you are leading American troops in Vietnam.

You have since learned how to drive.

And ...courtesy of the US Army ... you have learned how to kill.

And now it's payback time for scaring the hell out of your family. Which never really recovered from this experience.

The only good Communist/NVA is a dead Communist/NVA.

Lessons learned the hard way:

The NVA invariably attack on two occasions:

a.   When they're ready.
b.   b. When you're not.

Corollary:

It's hard to be macho when dust, dirt and gravel are flying up your nose from receiving incoming machine gun fire.

Sere

#Veteranslikeus: PTSD Symptoms In Combat Soldiers
Chapter 15

Once upon a time in a time and place far far away, there was a very young boy whose father was in the US Army Engineer Reserves. For training purposes, his unit was sent to Japan and so the boy and his mother stayed in the United States.

While the unit was in Japan, the North Koreans attacked South Korea.

The Engineer Company, including the boy's father were hastily thrown in battle as infantry (hours after they were called to active duty by the President).

The boy and his mother read about his father in the newspaper accounts of the day. He was a hero. And the boy continued to faithfully paste photographs and medals and newspaper clippings into the scrapbook that he had started while waiting for the day his father came home.

Then one day the father stood at the door to the apartment where the mother and son lived.

And all were happy.

As so it was that the father decided to stay in the U.S. Army and was transferred to West Germany. The boy knew that Communists were trying to kill his father in Korea. The boy hated Communists.

When the boy moved to West Germany, he saw there were many displaced people who lost their family/homes during WWII and they lived in refugee camps. They were hungry. They wore old coats and wrapped feet in rags because some did not have shoes. Some were children. Many were beggars on the street who would knock on the door and ask for work or bread. And the boy's mother would do what she could. The bombed out buildings with rubble still in them was where these people lived because the refugee camps were vastly overcrowded.

It happened that one day the boy asked the father "Why don't these people go back home?"

And the father replied "They can't because the Communists took over their land and government so that is why the US Army and I are here so the Communists don't take over more people".

The boy asked his father " Is that why you were in Korea?" And the father replies "Yes".

So the boy thought about this for a long long time.

Then one day ...at the dinner table ...the boy announces that he is going to be an infantry officer and kill Communists. Just like his father.

The boy went to the library and devoured books on famous battles in history along with interviews with famous soldiers and general military history. The boy also loved Mighty Mouse and Donald Duck comic books, joined the Cub and Boy Scouts and rode his bicycle and played soldier with his friends and at night, before he went to sleep, he immersed himself in his ever-growing library of US Army field manuals on hand-to-hand combat, adjusting artillery fire, how to recognize Soviet bloc uniforms, aircraft, tanks and much much more.

The boy's mother was not pleased. But the boy persisted in expanding his knowledge by listening to his father play poker on Friday nites and eavesdropping on the inevitable war stories that each participant told the other players. Stories that they didn't tell their wives or children.

The boy grew into a thin, skinny teenager who dated sporadically, ran track, played varsity football and competed in high school varsity wrestling. He had outgrown wrestling with his dad by applying what he had learned in hand-to-hand combat and his father was no longer a challenge.

One day in the young man's life ...there came the opportunity to use all of the accumulated wisdom from his years of preparation.

One day, in resting after a firefight, the boy who had matured into a man said to himself, "Only man does this."

Using some of the skills learned as a young boy at his father's side in hunting wild boar with a .45 pistol bought the young man home.

The man's friends had moved on while he was away. So the man kept to himself and got immersed in a new career. But he was lonely. He felt that he was a stranger in his home land. He talked to nobody about anything of importance because he had nothing to say. And some of those who thought they knew him told him he was weird.

Eventually the man met and married a wonderful woman and they had three kids. But the kids weren't allowed to play with or make guns out of their toys. In fact, the man did not tell his children that he had ever been on a battlefield until one day he was in a situation that he couldn't control and was involuntary put in a mental ward of a hospital for 10 days. Initially, the doctor treating him didn't know what was wrong until his wife mentioned that piece of the puzzle that had gone unnoticed to the untrained eye.

The years of flashbacks and unpleasant memories had finally caught up with the man who now had no choice but to tell his wife and children about some of his earlier experiences. Doctors told him that physical changes had occurred in his brain. Some of his circuits were "firing" incorrectly.

So the man began to take medications to restore the chemical imbalances in his brain.

Family and friends rallied around him and his family by lending comfort and support the best way they knew how. But that was not enough.

The man continues on a slow downward spiral despite the best medical care available.

Not all fables have a happy ending. This one does not.

Needless to say, this story is true and the boy is me. I was 8 years old when I joined the US Army.

If you are out in the boonies, it is absolute guarantee that something on your body aches, hurts, sore throbs, pinches or stings at any given time. Jump out of a hovering helicopter with a 60 pound pack and weapon and land wrong on your hands and feet and you feel the effects for days. Talk to your medic (nicely) and maybe you will get an aspirin for a bruised knee or scraped elbow.

So you learn to live with it.

Get into a firefight and it doesn't matter if you have stomach cramps from the heat or headache from the rain or you feel an asthma attack coming on. Or you have diarrhea or constipation.

It doesn't matter.

Your survival depends on the other people in your unit doing their assigned jobs at any given time. Their survival means you doing your assigned job. No matter how you feel ...or however your body is hurt, cut, bruised, cut, scraped or strained. It doesn't matter.

In a previous (#Veteranslikeus: PTSD Symptoms In Combat Soldiers , I asked: "Since this is the Christmas Season, I would like a Christmas present from you. It doesn't cost money. I have all the toys I need. But it does require a bit of your time.

For the past eleven months, you have read my thoughts and feelings on a variety of Vietnam and post Vietnam experiences that I had. I would like your reflection on the eleven updates that tells me how these stories have affected you.

 1)Has it opened the door for your family/friends to share some of their military experiences with you?

 2)When you see a Vietnam Vet in the news, has your opinion shifted in any way from a year ago?

 I ask that you find/make the time to respond. And not just leave it to others to answer these two questions.

 Because your answer means a lot to me."

As of , I received two responses answering these two questions. I realize that everybody has busy lives but all of December, January, February and March seems to me more than adequate for finding/making the time for something that absolutely meant a lot to me.

For me, the answer to these two questions IS the centerpiece of the documentary.

Because this newsletter is the documentary ...in print.

In #Veteranslikeus: PTSD Symptoms In Combat Soldiers #1), I received six responses out of the 22 e-mailed. In #Veteranslikeus: PTSD Symptoms In Combat Soldiers # 15), I received six out of 47 e-mailed.

Not surprisingly, it is invariably the same six people who respond every month.

Therefore, this is the last #Veteranslikeus: PTSD Symptoms In Combat Soldiers .

Those who contributed money will get a copy of the documentary when it is finished. My apologies to those six.

Sere

Since I wrote the above paragraphs, I been musing about keeping the option open of continuing #Veteranslikeus: PTSD Symptoms In Combat Soldiers if I receive enough specific answers to these two questions by this Sunday April 8.

I would like to hear from at least 9 of the 47 people on this list.

It's up to you.

Chapter 17

"Dear Dr. "X":

Sere has given me permission to contact you over some concerns that I have flowing from his session with you last Monday. We spent a few hours on Monday night/Tuesday morning talking about his session with you. I know he expressed to you his unhappiness, depression and I would say even despair, that his life is not what he would like it to be.

You suggested that he use part of his retroactive payment to buy a new "toy" that captures his interest. His response was that he is not interested in very many things these days.

From my perspective, I don't think a new toy will help much. What I see with Sere is that all the meds he takes suppress his emotions so much that he finds it difficult to explore things that might interest him. I know that he needs the meds so he is in a Catch-22 situation.

Additionally, his agoraphobia makes it difficult to pursue new interests. When out with people, he worries about saying or doing inappropriate things because the meds seem to impair his judgment. But I think that the most difficult problem to overcome is his rage.

Most of the time he is wound up tighter than a drum, trying to control his negative feelings (the meds don't do it all and if he took any more he would probably be a zombie). He invests so much of his energy over controlling his anger, feelings of betrayal, guilt over not "getting his men home" from Vietnam, and hostility toward any perceived enemy that he has no energy left to enjoy life. He is afraid that if he "lets go" he will hurt himself or others.

When he was in the research therapy group with the facilitator (Mr. X), I was able to listen to the audio tape of "his" session. When others in the group started to respond to his story, he deflected the support and tried to be there for the others. Even the facilitators kept reminding him that it was his turn to be supported.

His current group makes him more depressed because of his sense of responsibility toward everyone and his inability to help them.

What I think he needs is enough time and a safe place to let out the anger, rage, guilt, sadness and grief over what and whom he lost in Vietnam. Is there a way that he could be admitted to in patient care for a few weeks with individual therapy (he doesn't need any more groups to be responsible for)? He seems willing to try just about anything to turn his life around and he seemed to agree with what I was saying on Monday night.

I know he is also concerned about my smoking and weight and has expressed his concern to you. I am not trying to justify my own actions but I too find it difficult to look forward to any kind of joyful future. Sere gave me a two day trip to Yosemite for Christmas, but he won't go with me. We can't plan on concerts or theater together because he is never sure from one day to the next what his "status" will be. I married him because he is my best friend and lover and I want to share the important things in my life with him. My depression and its cause are certainly no way as severe as his but are just as real.

I've given up my group because Concord is just too far to go and there are no groups closer to home. So my support system has kind of collapsed. Friends and family try to be there for me, but it gets old talking to them about things they have no understanding of. It is difficult to get excited about life and plan for the future in our current situation.

I look forward to your insights and response.

Sincerely,

Stephanie Wilde"

The Vietnam Vet program continues at Channel 26 in Pacifica with 11 episodes to date. The stories come from nurses to sailors to medics to grunts. Some laugh on camera. Some cry. Thank you, America.

You are sound asleep because you have been up half the night. It is 6:45 A.M. The telephone rings. Stephanie answers because I don't answer the phone. You overhear the conversation between your older son and her saying that "A plane has hit the World Trade Center in New York!"

You think "Why is he calling to tell us that?"

So both of you go back to sleep.

You get up at 8:30 A.M. Take some meds. Fire up the computer and are startled to see the news bulletins about the planes deliberately hitting the World Trade Center.

You go to the TV and sit there glued to Peter Jennings.

For the first few hours of television footage of the burning buildings, you watch as your memories take over as you see people jump out of the windows ...and you remember helicopters exploding in the air and watching the body parts fall to the ground.

Undoubtedly some of the readers of #Veteranslikeus: PTSD Symptoms In Combat Soldiers are experiencing varying amounts of sadness, fear and despair as they open their mail, make plans to take airplane trips or watch their kids go off to school.
Eventually, most will put those emotions that surfaced on September 11 and bury them deep in the mind.

Most, but not all.

For WWII, Korean and Vietnam Veterans with PTSD, today is a version of September 11.

As it was yesterday.

And it will be tomorrow.

Until we die.

Welcome to our world of PTSD.

You have an appointment with your Nurse-Practitioner on the second floor. You enter the main entrance and stroll past the Volunteer Desk in the main corridor. On the left is the emergency room but the VA in its wisdom calls it "Evaluations and Assessments".
It has 37 seats.

I know because I have sat there and counted them while listening/talking to other vets and waiting for my appointment to begin.

(Of course, like any hospital emergency room, not everybody is there for the same thing. But while you are there, conversations flow between vets on: where can I get a shower, I only have $2.00 do you think they will let me get something to eat in the cafeteria, I wish it would stop raining.

And then there are those conversations between well-dressed vets ...about nightmares ..about drug/alcohol trips ...about time spent in county/state/Federal jails .. about divorces ... about estranged children/parents/relatives ..about in-country experiences that make some eavesdroppers vomit right on the spot.)

Just past the "Evaluations and Assessment" area off the main corridor is a room marked "GA-200 Life Support Unit - Staff Only".

Almost always, the door is closed. But occasionally, I go past while the door is slightly open. Invariably what I see is somebody in street clothes lying on a gurney with several people tending to or standing over somebody.

I don't stop and stare. If they are about my age, I wonder if I know them? Were they in-country when I was there? To think they went through all of the experiences they had ...only to die surrounded by strangers.

And then I remember. This is the reason I am here. To give voice to Vietnam Veterans to say those things that need to be said so that members of future generations will not need to write a #Veteranslikeus: PTSD Symptoms In Combat Soldiers or produce a documentary.

I have way too many memories of bending over and caring for my people when they were in a bad way. And I have memories of my people bending over and caring for me when I was in a bad way.

Remembering those I cared about laying on the ground with their knees flapping together, their arms flopping from side-to-side and unearthy sounds at the top of their lungs with pink foam coming out of their mouths ...makes me very quiet and moody for days.

And rekindles anew fires of rage at those bored by these experiences.

Sere

Lesson learned the hard way:
The density of fire coming at you increases proportionally the closer you get to NVA positions..

Chapter 18

Just after I finished the previous #Veteranslikeus: PTSD Symptoms In Combat Soldiers , I was preparing a sizable mailing for KMVT 15 Silicon Valley Community Media – Mountain View. As it happened, I was sitting alone in a back room when all of a sudden, the power went out ...leaving me alone in the darkness.

Just before I had time to get upset and overreact, the power went back on.

But I didn't go back to finishing the mailing.

I went and sat in another office until the Assistant General Manager peeked in and asked "Is everything OK?"

It wasn't. And I knew it. I had been down this road before.

I was mentally exhausted from the efforts to get guests for each month's Vietnam Vet show. Fatigue that regularly puts me into bed almost immediately after each show had set in. And this strain had been building on me for months. Fatigue that told me that something had to give.

So I talked with my psychiatrist about whatever benefits I was supposedly getting from putting myself through this every month. It was time to take a breather and rethink not only the TV show but also the documentary. Both were on the line.

It is dark. Another firefight. Rapid, intense flashes of light sputter at you from several car lengths away ...splintering the bamboo around you.

Machine guns fire, grenades explode and rifles bark. The longest minute of your life is taking place. Your men/you and the NVA are swapping hostilities and vigorously trying to out-flank each other. Maneuvering is from very close range. Vietnamese and American voices scream in fear.
You are doing the ultimate in hide-and-seek ... in a flat and dry rice paddy ... the size of a baseball field. And both sides are getting hurt.

You earn $399.30 a month. Before taxes. Milk is $1.26 a gallon. And while you are upSereing from heat exhaustion, back in the world (USA), people are settling in to watch" Rowan & Martin's Laugh-In" and "Dragnet" on television.

And you would be more than happy just to see the Sun come over the horizon just one more time

It is time to break contact. You radio your Platoon Sergeant at the other end of your unit and both of you simultantaneously cut loose with an 18 round clip of red tracer ammunition into the middle of the NVA.

A "Bird Dog" (Cessna 150) finally arrives directly over your location. Two grenade launchers fire two white phosperous (canisters that burn at 1500 degrees Farenheit) grenades to mark the front of the NVA position and then two more rounds to mark the rear of the NVA position.

Almost immediately, you hear the whine of two (F-4) Phantoms snaking just above the tree tops and beginning their strafing gun. Your troops move away from the NVA in small groups while being exceedingly cautious that you do not stumble into an ambush set up behind you.

As you pop behind a tree to deliver covering fire for your men who are withdrawing, two NVA pop out of a bamboo thicket behind you ...with the intent ... on using you for bayonet practice.

The Radio-Telephone Operator behind you catches their movement and cuts them down with a full burst from his M-16.

Another session of hell on Earth is here.

Again.

Hand-to-hand fighting begins to take place in the darkness. The noises of feet scrambling, high pitched American and Vietnamese voices groaning and grunting, bones and necks are snapping and ribs caving in ... mingle ... with the sound of another two Phantom jets coming in for another pass.

Americans at home are preparing for another peace rally. Others are putting bumper sticks on their car saying "America Love It ...Or Leave It".

The surge of adrenaline within you gives an instant headache. Your knuckles are bleeding and sore as hell. Your ribs hurt and now you have a knife wound sizzling in your right forearm.

There is no Jacuzzi.

But you are alive.

And for the rest of your life ...the headaches you now get ... literally knock you to your knees as they always remind you of the kill-or-be-killed in hand-to-hand combat.
It is one thing to drop a bomb from an airplane going 400 miles an hour. It is another thing to fire an artillery shell at a target up to 7 miles away.

And it something else indeed to kill with just your hands, feet and legs.

And even though it has been 33 years, Stephanie and Robert and Daniel will learn about the knife wound for the first time when they read this.

Several readers say that my writing moves them sometimes to tears/anger/frustration.

My purpose is informing readers about what it is like to have combat related PTSD on a daily basis.

Or to live with those who do.

Plenty of people in the US, besides combat veterans, have PTSD. Some work/live in and around the World Trade Center, others are rape victims, survivors of traffic accidents, childhood abuse sufferers, emergency care workers as in doctors - nurses - paramedics - cops or prostitutes and refugees.

But this is about writing and not PTSD in particular. Writing a #Veteranslikeus: PTSD Symptoms In Combat Soldiers takes me between 6 to 10 hours over several weeks. Depending upon how much of the daily meds I take, an issue takes shape in 15 to 40 minute segments. Then I go to sleep. And when I awake, I do something else.

Writing updates is not something that I like to do nor does it come easy to me.

But then again ...writing letters home to wives and parents didn't come easy either. There isn't the luxury of a few weeks to prepare one. For example, for a soldier is killed in action, US Army protocol calls for the soldier's commander to write his next-of-kin.

Ideally, this letter is written as soon as possible after the soldier's death. But in a combat situation ...that is not always possible. In some units, there are clerks who job includes writing this letter.

But not in mine.

Out in the boonies, there are no typewriters.

So ...we would get blank writing paper and envelopes on which we did not have to pay postage. We just wrote "FREE" in the upper right hand corner of the envelope, addressed it and sent it on its way. When a helicopter would make a supply drop or ammo drop ...even in a firefight ...it was common to see somebody rush up to the door gunner and hand him a stack of envelopes as they unloaded supplies. I often wonder to this day ...how many vets died in trying to get to a helicopter under fire just so they could send a letter home.

It is Monday. You have another 9:00 appointment with a psychologist specializing in treating hatred and phobias. You also have your regular 3:00 group meeting with fellow PTSD vets. It is easier on all concerned if you just stay at Ft. Miley all day instead of traveling back and forth.

Of course, if you drove ...

So you spend your time wandering over the hospital grounds. You go buy a cup of chocolate in the cafeteria. You go sit in "Assessments & Evaluations" (Emergency Room). You go over to Building 8 (Psych Building) and sit downstairs in the waiting room.

Ultimately getting bored of this little dance, you sit in the lobby of the Main Entrance and people watch. The Residents from UC-San Francisco Med School in their white coats, stethoscopes tossed around their neck and over their shoulder and walking at a fast pace. You watch the aged father struggling up the ramp with his cane as his wife and grown-up daughter walk behind him encouraging his every step.

As he enters Building 208, you and others notice that he is wearing a gold-and-white braided cap that says "Bataan Death March Survivor". Conversations in the lobby stop. People crowded around the Information Desk instantly part so that he has a barrier free corridor to walk through.

Conversation resumes as the Filipino veteran disappears down the hallway.

A furiously angry vet comes running out of the Assessments and Evaluations. He stops at the Information Desk and profanely cusses out at the clerk sitting there about the two hour wait he has endured to get his meds. Which he still doesn't have.

Wheelchair vet rumbles down the hallway. He is missing his right leg. He stops in front of your chair and wheels around to watch others coming and going out of the Main Entrance. 10 minutes later, he puts his hands on the wheels, spins around and looks you directly in the eyes. You return his stare with a smile. His body softens as he returns your smile.

You think that you can't do this on Monday anymore.
So you walk down the hallway to the Cafeteria.

There is a crowd around the ATM machine. A vet with two hooks for hands is feverishly trying to extract a dollar bill from his wallet for the Coke machine next to the ATM. You offer to help. He says "Just give me a moment, I can do this". Finally he does so.

You continue on to the Cafeteria.

Your stomach goes berserk. A scream that began 32 years ago begins at your toes and rises to your throat like a volcano about to explode. You feel a need to pound a fist through the walls. It takes every iota of willpower that you can muster not to scream at the top of your lungs. Tears flow until you remember to take a deep breath. Everything will be OK. Just take a deep deep breath.

You will be here next Monday.

Just like you were here last Monday.

And then one day there won't be any more Monday's.

You will be home with those you loved ...who will always be forever young ...with their names etched on a Wall in Washington DC..

Thank you America

Some time ago, I was asked if anybody wore/carried "lucky charms". At that particular moment, I couldn't remember. It has been a while. But then it came to me.

I did.

Literally, just before I got on the plane, Stephanie gave me a small crucifix even though our religions differ. I put it in my pocket and promptly forgot about it. Later, after I had been in-country for a while, I lost it when we were in ambush position for the night. Just before we were to break out of our night position, I discovered that I had lost it. Next thing I knew, there were 17 people including myself keeping our eyes pealed for the NVA that were looking for us and searching for the crucifix.

Somebody found it.

I never lost it again.

When I came home, I told Stephanie about it. Since we were about to get married. She took it to a jewelry store on Clement Street in San Francisco and asked the owner what could he do to make it into a wedding ring set. Somehow he did. And that is the wedding ring that she and I both have.

Only now, she wears hers.

Ultimately, the wedding ring didn't do me any favors. So I don't wear mine.

At 13th and Mission Streets in San Francisco is the Vet Center. This location is a mini Ft. Miley with a primary focus of screening medical needs of vets. Some have PTSD. Some have alcohol and drug problems. Some have these issues and more.

One Monday a month, I see a PTSD orientated psychiatrist who shuttles between work locations at 13th Street and Ft. Miley. On this particular day, I am waiting for the 2:15 PM shuttle van to take me to Ft. Miley for another appointment. Standing, around the 5 bench seat passenger van, are some sullen vets waiting for the driver to make his appearance so we can leave.

Nobody says a word except to bum a cigarette. Hands are stuffed in pockets to ward off the cold. Some wear bulky jackets hiding rail thin bodies. The driver, an affable sort ... is a substitute for the regular driver, appears and unlocks the doors so all 15 of us can climb in.

The van is quiet as the driver speeds out Fell Street along the Panhandle into Golden Gate Park. Jogging on the path along the Strybing Arboretum and Botanical Gardens are several attractive young women in sweats and baseball caps complete with their pony-tails bouncing rhythmically behind them.

Driver comes to the stop sign. A bevy of beauties cross the road in front of the van and the driver starts a commentary about their appearance.

I am sitting in the last seat in the back of the van.

In the seat in front of me, a vet stops staring at his feet and yells "Will you shut the fuck up and just drive the goddam bus?"

The driver's voice trails off.

It becomes absolutely dead silent.

A height challenged vet sitting beside me makes his way up to the driver and says" If you don't drive this fucking thing so I can make my appointment on time, I am going to kick your ass right here and now."

Claps and whistles rattle through the van as the driver makes it to Ft. Miley ... in record time.

Another example of relatively young men grown old before their time. Life and most of its pleasures ...are ... just ...words in the dictionary.

Subsequently, this substitute driver is reassigned because of threats to his safety.

It is November 13th. It is Job Fair day at San Francisco State.

You and the PCT General Manager are here to recruit interns for the forthcoming semester. For this purpose, you get there at 9:30 AM for the 10:00 AM opening so that you have the best table for meeting and greeting the incoming students looking for their first job upon graduation.

It is a lot of fun. Most of the students have that zest for adventure in the business world and it becomes contagious as you hand out brochures and talk one-on-one with film and broadcast students.

Since you were here last year doing the same thing, the feeling of panic is not as intense. Even though crowds of students fill the room and spill over past your table out into the hallway and stairs.

Toward the close of the day, you are in particularly intense give-and-take discussion with one student about the treadmill of producing your own program for television. And in particular, Vietnam Vet.

From behind you comes a small voice with the question "Did I overhear you say Vietnam?"

The question is repeated: "Did I overhear you say Vietnam?"

The student you are talking to quickly finishes his conversation, takes some literature and moves on to the next exhibition table.

Moving directly to where the previous student stood is now a very young Asian student and takes upon himself to say for the third time in a flawless American accent : "Did I overhear you say Vietnam?"

33 years of irritation begins to boil as this young man with brown eyes and jet black hair says "I am a Operation Babylift baby. I was four weeks old when the orphanage I was in ... put me and my sister on a plane to America. I don't know who my biological parents are. I don't even know where to start."

This kid is on a roll.

"We flew into Travis Air Force Base and ultimately, my sister and I were adopted by an American family in Wisconsin." "I would give anything if I have family back in Vietnam. Who they were and how my sister and I end up in the orphanage"

I haven't said a word since he began this conversation.

It's been 49 years since I have touched a Vietnamese.

Which I had to kill.

This one I had to hug.

And, I did.

And cried.

For him and me.

Signed:

Sere

PS: Operation Babylift was a last ditch effort by World Airways to bring out (for free) as many mixed race babies of American/Vietnamese origin as they could in the hours just before the NVA took over.

One such plane (C5A - Galaxy) overflowing with 400+ babies and young children was hit by a NVA rocket as it was sitting on the runway outside Saigon waiting for takeoff. The last American woman- Mary Therese Klinker - killed in Vietnam (April 4th 1975) was on that plane.

There is no justification for deliberately targeting a rocket on a cargo plane filled with children.

None.

Bastards.

Chapter 18

It's Monday. Your regular combat PTSD group meeting is about to begin.

Stephanie is parked outside the trailer where your meeting takes place.

You enter the meeting room. The facilitator tells you that a surgical patient who is just recovering from major surgery can attend the meeting but that someone from the group will have to go to his bedside and then wheel him down the sidewalk, across the parking lot and up the ramp for the 90 minute meeting.

You never left anybody behind in Vietnam. You are not going to leave anybody today ...in a different battlefield.

So you and another vet literally run out of the meeting room to his bedside. He has got IV tubes and catheters stuck everywhere. White hospital bandages sprinkle about his chest and arms.

He is uncomfortable. You start to feel a little uneasy. Memories surface. Screaming to the point of hoarseness. Bandages that you have to wrap and tie together like a shoelace. Blood everywhere. Helicopters. Rifle shots.

It is starting to rain.

Your stomach spasms as you tell yourself "That was then. This is now!!!"

Somewhere along the way, you become the officer again and now this is one of your wounded men you are grunting/groaning to a spot where the Dustoff can pick him up.

You are on a mission.

The hospital bed is unwieldy. Even though it is on casters, it isn't made for wheeling down side walks and being pulled up parking lots angled to the top of a hill. You and the other vet helping are grunting and groaning because this bed and its patient are heavy. Very heavy. It starts to sprinkle. The water bottle in your jacket breaks open and completely drenches your leg.

Something bad is happening here.

You are in combat. Instinctively, you keep low to the ground. Your head is on a swivel looking for threats. The rain has now become sweat pouring off of you. You don't have a weapon because it is just too hard for two people to push/pull/lift/shove a wounded man and use a weapon at the same time.

Normal traffic noise coming from Muni buses and cars merge into the "whoop-de-whoop" of the waiting helicopter waiting to lift your man out of harms way. Sounds of a brief firefight echo through your head.

You accomplish your mission. That's what the US Army pays you to do.

In the meeting itself, you literally say not a word.

Another vet has a bigger need.

And, as Stephanie watched through her windshield, she saw her husband in combat

The Monday PTSD group fellow Vietnam Vet in the bed?

?Here are extracts from his PTSD claim filed last November with the Veterans Administration ...

"I came into the Air Force on August 3rd, 1964, the day after the Gulf of Tonkin Incident with a Lincoln Nebraska upbringing and world view: I was a Boy Scout. I had a paper route. I played varsity football and was on the debate team. I had the world's prettiest girlfriend.

After 30 months of training, I spent 1 year, 5 months and 9 days as part of a forward observer team trained to fight against Soviet Union's SAM-2 missile defense systems throughout Southeast Asia. I am 20 years old.

Extract of 2 Stressful Incidents:

17:) The Long Walk:
Near Xom Kieu, October 9th 1967, we split the team to tackle a dual SAM site operation, my squad subsequently was ambushed during the helicopter insertion and before we broke off engagement with the NVA, our only radio was damaged beyond repair. We spent the next 18 days sneaking into Ban Nape (Laos) where we ran into a Marine Recon unit and were finally extracted.

24:) The Pickup
Coming to the rescue of another team downed by a Rocket Propelled Grenade, near Muang Thathorn(Laos) April 22nd 1968, my team was faced with this situation:
We had one helicopter and 21 men to extract. I was second in charge, except for the other team leader, Capt (name withheld in this publication for reasons of privacy), who was hit and bleeding to death. We got 18 of the men out of there, but we had to leave three behind including the Capt.

To a civilian, 18 out of 21, especially with a helicopter built to carry 9, would seem to be a successful operation, but within the discipline and tradition of a combat unit, it is a failure, a violation of the code. And I was the presiding officer over that failure.

To attempt to bring out the other three meant that we would have had to stand and fight; except that this was such a well-coordinated ambush in which we could not stand and fight. I made a "sensible" and a tactically responsibile decision, and 35 years later, the bitterness of it all still has the ability to make me swallow hard..

Is it stressful ...if the instances of stress live with you for 35 years and continue to remind you of a time/place where things in your life were out-of-control?

Losing a pilot and aircraft during the pre-Vietnam training period was STRESSFUL.

Interrogating a Russian-speaking Vietnamese national was STRESSFUL.

Sitting deep in the bowels of a RB-47 (reconnaissance aircraft) and waiting for the Electronic Warefare Office to correctly turn aside a SAM missile that had acquired us as a target was STRESSFUL
Look at my employment history - 27 jobs in 10 years or my tenant/renter history or my banking history. For the past 15 years, it would be hard to find a landlord, banker or employer who had anything good to

say about me. My friends of old are now distant memories. I have not seen one of my them in over 20 years. And then there is the crazy stuff such as driving without a license for 18 years. For most of the past 20 years, any friends at all have been Vietnam Veterans, and as with the current batch, I have never been to one of their homes nor they mine.

My psychiatrist tell me I am now "unemployable". My range of emotions go from Angry-Tired-Scared. "Intrusive thoughts" are just the regular working of my brain. I feel extreme anxiety. I feel hopelessness and I have a curious ability to have chills and fever at the same time.

Influenced by hallucinations, I have placed cups on tables that are not there, eaten mouthfuls of non-existent food and there are signs that my PTSD is growing more powerful.

Every day, the news, personal encounters, literature and memories return me to Vietnam with some reference or gesture. It just never goes away. And the scary thing is: This is as good as it gets."

{{Editorial Note: The author of the above passage does not swear/smoke or do drugs. Never did. His wife died several years ago. Two adult children live in the Mid-West and have no idea that, within the past year, he has been both homeless and almost evicted from a studio apartment in a run-down hotel in the Mission District. His only source of income is Social Security Disability Insurance }}

More of the slang:

Numbah-One GI: serviceman who spends a good deal of money on the Vietnamese economy.

Numbah-Ten GI: serviceman who spends little money in the Vietnamese economy.

Nuoc Mam: the Vietnamese national dish consisting of fermented fish sauce.

Plenty Cheap Charlie: one who wastes even less money than an ordinary cheap charlie.

P's: piastres; basic Vietnamese monetary unit. $1 equals 118 piastres.

Punji Stick: sharpened bamboo stick planted in the ground at 45 degree angle with the point sticking up. Almost always smeared with shit becoming a fast acting poison in the bloodstream.

Real Life civilian life. As in, "Hey, Lieutenant what do you do in Real Life, ?"

Rice Wine: an alcoholic drink made from rice. Tastes like kerosene.

Rog: short for "Roger," the radio term for "I understand your transmission.

Roundeye: Caucasian woman.

Saigon Tea: sometimes soda purchased in thimble-size glasses as the price of a hostess' company in a bar. The hostess gets a commission, and she will drink as many as the customer can buy, as fast as he will buy them.

With 2.8 million Americans serving in the Vietnam War, it is a serious blunder to think that any one veteran (including me) speaks for all (or the majority of) the veterans of that war.

Several months ago, I find myself helping to film a September 11 Memorial Service to be shown later on . The ceremony is taking place in a open field. A local veterans organization is leading the honor guard and flag bearers to the podium.

As I watch all the big and small flags flapping in the wind for the ceremony, I kept coming back to the memory of an American soldier covering himself with a six foot long American flag to mark his position on the ground to the Forward Air Controller overhead in a slow flying airplane.

That soldier burned to death from a napalm strike overflowing from the NVA bunker onto him. I watch him and the American flag envelope into a white-hot ball of flame bigger than your car.

From 50 feet away. Burning human flesh, loudest scream I have ever heard in my life. Smell that stopped me from eating barbecued hamburgers for years and years.

It is safe to wear the American flag on your lapel, bumper sticker it to your car or hang it in the window. It is a tremendous act of courage to wave it when somebody is actively shooting at you.

From 50 feet away.

He died. I didn't. God only knows why.

Don't wave the flag in front of me.

Chapter 19

The sleep of your bone-tired infantry platoon in a night defensive position, already exhausted by day upon day upon day of 100 degree plus heat while carrying 60 pound packs, is now interrupted by the sudden blinding flash of a trip-wire flare announcing the immediate presence of about 40 NVA running towards you. From 50 feet away.

You wake and immediately know that these are going to be your last seconds on Earth. Thoughts of "Will I ever see my wife, brother, sisters or Mom or Dad again" flash through your mind.

NVA pop up behind you and attack your position simultaneously from two different directions as your infantry platoon suddenly awakens from the noise and light to defend itself from this NVA unit fully intent on killing every American they see or hear.

Machine gun, rifle and pistol shots mix with hand-to-hand combat break out as the organized assault turns into a free-for-all. Soldiers on both sides die from gunshots and rifle butts to the face, bayonet wounds to the stomach as well as steel helmet smashes to the top of the head.

14 hours of hand-to-hand combat instruction in basic training now has life and death consequences for those who paid attention during training. And, in this rice field, there are no points awarded for the proper execution of a strike, parry or blocking maneuver or flying kicks to the head nor over-the-shoulder throws as in the martial arts movies. Biting, eye-gouging, head-butting, spine-stomping, ball-grabbing, hair-pulling and rabbit punching is the order of the day.

Groups of two's, three's or more gang up on one individual for the quick kill and move on to the next opponent.

Theirs. Ours.

You always sleep alongside one of the two M-60 machine guns in your unit. The gunner, who was sound asleep when the assault began, finally clears an ammunition jam and begins spewing out death.

Your Radio-Telephone-Operator, sleeping in another part of the defensive position, can't get to your location but follows standard-operating-procedure and quickly informs headquarters that your unit is now engaged in hand-to-hand combat with a numerically superior NVA force and requests assistance.

You drag a wounded man to a more protected location with one hand and fire your AK-47 with the other hand when suddenly another blinding flare goes off in front of you and now you see, for the first time ever ....your NVA counterpart crouching with one knee on the ground and using toots on his whistle while flashing arm-and-hand signals. His Radio-Telephone-Operator is right behind him yelling into the phone. Both of them are, maybe, 75 feet away.

You let go of your wounded man and ,with both hands now holding the AK-47 and shaking all over the place, empty a full magazine into them. 30 minutes later, you are methodicaly going through their pockets/backpacks on their still warm bodies searching for any maps, letters, insignia, pictures that might have value in saving American/Vietnamese lives.

You know they would do the same to you.

And, during this 30 minute period, you gain first-hand knowledge that if you survive a hand-to-hand encounter your arms and legs will throb in pain, your chest and stomach will be on fire and your lungs desperate for anything close to a deep breath.

If you don't survive the hand-to-hand, you don't feel anything because you are dead.

Flash forward 32 years and your therapist suggests you find a way to see the Vietnamese not only as NVA but also as innocent husbands, wives, children, grandparents, uncles and aunts suffering all the hardships of war and having no connection to the NVA.

It takes me several years to reach this conclusion. A year ago, I put a picture of very young Vietnamese toddlers above my bed so that I can see it everyday. On occasion, I take a friend or Stephanie to a Vietnamese restaurant several blocks from my home. I didn't know that the Vietnamese diet is big on fish and soups in addition to rice. Because where I was, there were no roadside vendors, cafes, restaurants and very, very few villages.

In fact, the only Vietnamese food that I ever ate came from grabbing a handful of whatever was in the cooking pots sitting over the campfires in the NVA positions that we overran.

The Vietnamese that I came into contact with were doing their best to kill me. And my men.

I have a 10HP 3-Phase motor left over from my small business. It would be perfect for lifting water or running an air compressor to power small tools. I wanted to send it to a village in South Vietnam.

Eventually, I came into contact with an American organization that provides life saving assistance directly to rural Vietnamese people and sent the following email:

...I am a Vietnam Vet on disability with PTSD from the VA. Is it possible to "adopt" a Vietnamese family through your organization? I still don't like the Vietnamese government but I don't have anything against the Vietnamese people.

So my wife and I would like to help one family financially for our remaining lifetimes. I am not interested in returning to RVN but I would like to reach out and help the healing.

Any information along these lines would be very highly appreciated.

Signed:

Sere ...

And this is the response that I received

""Hi Sere,

Thank you for the email and interest in "XXX". Yes, "XXX" has a "Family Sponsorship Program". I have attached a brief description for you.

In summary, the Family Sponsorship program identifies the most needy families in a hamlet.

Our social workers ascertain the best way to help the family. "XXX" does not give "cash handouts", because it sets a bad precedent and is not very effective. We purchase exactly what the family needs. Each family is different. One family may need food, while another needs to keep their kids in school. Another family may need a home.

We have many Vets associated with "XXX". I think that all of them have benefited from helping a Vietnamese family or child. Some have even returned to Viet Nam to meet the people they have helped ... a very emotional and moving experience.

The selection process is pretty intensive, as we had more than 30 new families who were worthy of starting the program this year, yet we were only able to offer sponsorship to 10 right now.

Each family is first brought to our attention by the Vietnamese authorities. The families are then investigated and the list narrowed down to the selected 30 by Tung and Chi Huong, our 2 social workers. Our goal is to find families who are at a high risk for collapse, yet have a high potential to succeed and become self sufficient. These families are usually single parent families, with 2 or more children that may be forced to drop out of school out of necessity to earn a living.

Potentially life threatening health problems may or may not be present, but what is always present is hunger and malnutrition. "XXX" has a strict policy of "no cash handouts", because it is a very ineffective way to help a person. Therefore, we research what the family needs the most, and we purchase/pay for what is deemed most needed.

Thanks again for your care and concern towards the Pham family and all the people of Viet Nam.

Should you decide to make a donation, the following family has been selected to receive it.

FAMILY'S CIRCUMSTANCES:
In 1986, Mrs. Pham, her husband and their eldest son moved to a new residential area for living, in hopes of improving their life. In 1995, they moved back home, since the Vietnamese economy had improved some. However, they had to leave the eldest son with his grandparents at the new residential area because they found it impossible to provide for all 4 children.

After that, she discovered that her husband was having an affair with another woman and had 2 children with that woman. Her husband hit her badly after a very serious argument about the situation. He stabbed her with a big kitchen knife. It was an unpardonable offence. Her husband has been put into the prison from that time on.

After her husband was put into the jail, her family started a very hard life: no land for farming, no money, no job and their only source of income was gone. Because of her love for the children, she had to look past all the obstacles in life, to find a way out for her family. She learned how to make bloating rice cake (a Vietnamese traditional food) and peddled around the villages selling the cakes to earn money.

Although she worked all day long, she could not earn enough for living expenses and her children's school fees. She then rented a shop near her house and did processing work for rice cake. She is able to earn more, about $25 a month, but it is still not enough to provide for the 5 family members.

She still works very hard. She has to get up at 3:00 am to make rice cake and sells them up to 10:00 pm. After study time, her children help their mother with housework and selling the cakes at the shop. She wishes to have money to raise pigs for sale but she finds it impossible to find the money to make her simple wish come true.

All her 4 children are very good at school. They are aware of their mother's hardship and the difficulties in life that they have made their greatest efforts in their studies.

POSSIBLE RISKS:
In view of the above circumstance, Mrs. Pham's family has plenty of risks such as:
- Poverty and malnutrition threatens her family frequently
- Mrs. Pham is now overburdened with too many responsibilities. What happens if Mrs. Pham, the main income of the family falls sick?
- Mrs. Pham does not have enough money to afford living expenses and schooling fees for her 4 children.
- Her four children are good students but it is most certain that they will be forced to quit since Mrs. Pham cannot afford their school costs.

RATIONALE FOR THIS FAMILY TO BENEFIT FROM FAMILY SPONSORSHIP PROGRAM
- Ms. Pham is a hard-working and honest person, but the current situation makes their life so hard and impossible to find a way to improve her family's situation.
- She is person of good virtue, who takes good care of her children.
- Her four children are good students who need to be helped to have good education.
- Her family should be helped to have more opportunities for self-efficiency, since Mrs. Pham is very motivated to raise pigs.

RECOMMENDATIONS: $240 funded by Stephanie and Charles Bussey to be suggested to help Mrs. Pham's family for the whole year:
- Provide financial support of about $ 120 for the first 6 months to help lessen the financial burden of this family, by paying for school fees, nutritious food and other living expenses.
- Help the family with income-generating activities like pig raising so that Ms. Pham and her children can raise the pigs and sell them for more income
- Consider the needs of the family, and try to find good way to help improve the situation of the family so that they can lift themselves out of poverty.
-

~Written by Hoang Ngoc Tung, "XXX" social worker, DaNang office

1 The Pham Family # 1

2 The Pham Family # 2

Just a note: I read many of these reports, and this particular family's situation is much worse than the average report I have seen. In particular, they look quite malnourished and small. They will undoubtedly benefit from your help!"

One year later, I get the following report on our $240 contribution:

"Family Name:
Nguyen Pham
Danang, Vietnam

STATUS BEFORE FAMILY SPONSORSHIP
No money in the bank and no livestock. Children at risk of dropping out of school. Low nutrition level.

PROGRAM ACCOMPLISHMENT
Payment of 1 year's school fees for all children. Purchase of six piglets, pig food and pig rearing supplies.

STATUS AFTER ONE YEAR FAMILY SPONSORSHIP
Savings account of 1,000,000 VND ($65 USD) and ownership of 8 pigs. All four children are continuing in school. Improved nutrition.

PROGRAM PROGRESS:
Mrs. Pham was interested in raising pigs before we started the family sponsorship program and she learned very well. She raised the 6 piglets and sold 4 of them for USD76.48. After purchasing nutritious food for the family, she still saves USD65.00 to reinvest in the piglet business. She is currently raising another 6 piglets and owns 8 pigs total now. She has a good understanding of pig raising and will continue to work hard to have her business be successful for many years to come.

EFFECTS;
The income generated from raising and selling the pigs is enough to buy more nutritious food and to pay part of the children's school fees. The family has made good progress in these areas.

Thanks to the Family Sponsorship Program, her daughters no longer have to work very hard after school to help her sell rice cakes. The daughters have more time to focus on their studies and become good students this school year. All 4 children are committed to staying in school and they study very hard.

Mrs. Pham is very thankful to the donors and kindness towards her family.

RECOMMENDATION:
By her own efforts, she has worked very hard to improve her family's situation. However, there are still many difficulties awaiting her in coming time. She would benefit from another year in the Family Sponsorship program until she can raise herself above the poverty line. More specifically, she needs to afford more food, more nutritious food, and to pay for all 4 children to finish high school. "XXX" feels she will do that if given the chance."

Mrs. Pham was 2 years old when I got to Viet Nam

I wish Mrs. Pham and her 4 children every success in overcoming her challenges now and in the future and that her piglet raising business survives and thrives beyond measure.

May they never hear a shot fired in anger.

This update from "XXX" literally came in from Viet Nam yesterday:

"SOME INFORMATION OF MS. NGUYEN THI PHAM'S FAMILY (January 6th 2006)

Current Situation: Under the assistance of Stephanie and Charles Bussey, the life of Ms. Pham's family had been improving. At that time, she raised 8 pigs and tried to earn more income to afford her children to school. But then the life was getting more and more difficult and her family's financial condition gets harder as her children have grown up. She has to work hard to support their living and her children's schooling. She wished to raise more pigs to earn more income but she had to sell them to have money to afford the daily expenses.

Currently, due to the shortage of money, she can only buy 3 piglets to raise. After 4 months, she can earn USD$19 from selling the three pigs. Thus sum does not help her cover all living and education and education expenses for her family.

She must contrive to earn enough USD60 to pay the schooling for her four children who are in school. Monthly, the eldest son must pay about USD$31 for his study in carpentry and it takes about 3 months for him to finish his study in carpentry and after that he has to look for a job to earn a living.

Her elder daughter has to pay USD$15 for her schooling because she studies at 12th Grade and prepares for the next university entrance examination, she must pay USD$9.50 and USD$22 for her two last children who study at 10th and 9th grades respectively.

Ms. Pham must support meager meals and her children's schooling in a few ways: doing pig husbandry, hiring herself out as a hired farmer, or picking pennyworts. She can earn about USD$1.90 per day from these works. Even doing arduous works with all her efforts, her family still faces difficulties and lives in privation.

RECOMMENDATION

Mrs. Pham wishes that if she has a sum of money, she will raise sow. She thinks that his is the efficient way to make money and suitable with her health condition because one of the two hands was chopped off by her brutal husband.

Ms. Pham says that if she has enough money to buy a sow, she can earn up to USD$28 because she believes this sow can deliver baby pigs and she will keep some piglets to raise instead of buying them at the market.

It is kindly suggested that her family would have financial assistance with a sum of $300 per year so that she can raise 3 sows to generate her income because each year, one sow can deliver about 8 to 12 piglets. She earns money more efficiently and effectively from the incomings from this pig husbandry. By this way, the program can facilitate her children's education better and her living conditions will gradually improve much better."

Too bad that Ms. Pham's husband isn't old enough to be an NVA I came into contact with 37 years ago. The NVA/VC consistently stabbed and cut off the arms or buried village chiefs and their families alive as a way to intimidate villagers.

You and your seven Monday PTSD group members are standing outside the trailer right after the session ended.

One member happens to notice the POW emblem on the license plate on the SUV parked next to you.

Since you know that POW stands for "Prisoner of War", you turn around and ask the very elderly and frail driver "Which war?"

"WWII. Yeah, I'm Bataan Death March survivor"

So you shake his hand and say "Well, me, let me thank you for your service."

"WOW, I've never had anybody say "Thank you for my service".

You remember that 26,000 Americans were captured along with 50,000 Filipino troops by the Japanese in April 1942 and then were literally starved, beaten and worked to death until liberated in August 1945. Half died. The Japanese Commander was hanged for this war crime in 1946.

How do you feel about the Japanese today?

"Well, I don't harbor any animosity toward anybody."

Would you buy a Japanese product?

"Not if I can help it. My son-in-law bought a Toyota a long time ago. I've yet to ride in it. But I am not bitter."

Thank you again for your service to your country.

"You're welcome".

Members of the group get into their cars and head off to a local restaurant for a pre-arranged dinner.

No one says anything about the very elderly and frail driver.

Conversation among us at dinner is subdued. Unspoken is the thought that among our family, friends, neighbors and co-workers, even among the VA psychotherapists that treat us is the realization, just like that Bataan Death March survivor: "Nobody ever thanked me for my service to this country."

Or in my case, get told " ... I do not believe it's good for you to tell and in some cases repeat your story. Each time I hear your story it (to me) seems that you become more depressed. I believe it is time for you to leave your story behind and move on."

This sentiment is vastly outweighed by family members who arrange their day-to-day schedules to see that I always have $20 in my wallet, transportation to/from medical appointments (since I don't drive) and comfort during times of extreme stress.

This sentiment is also vastly outweighed by friends dear to me who: bake me sweet potato pies at Christmas, invite me into their homes on Tuesdays to spend the day when Stephanie/Robert/Daniel are away to work, look the other way when I burst into tears over a spontaneous combat memory, call me regularly just to say "Hello" or occasionally spend time waiting with me for appointments at Ft. Miley or even return my emails when they contain rants about the quality of my life and those around me.

But I have never forgotten the poem that I learned in high school:

God and the soldier, we adore
In time of danger, not before.
The danger past and all things righted,
God's forgotten, the soldier slighted.
- Rudyard Kipling -

Please be advised that what follows next is a rant. It is not written with animosity towards any past or current therapist or VA official. Without exception, each Veterans Administration therapist that I have come in contact with over the past 17 years has proven to me they have my best interest at heart.

But there is something that needs to be said if you are going to continue to look inside the daily life of a combat vet with severe PTSD.

This past January, I was invited to participate in a collaborative study between the VA and University of California San Francisco called "Open Trial of Cognitive-Behavioral-Therapy of Chronic PTSD in Vietnam Combat Veterans." This resulted in weekly and sometimes twice weekly one-on-one individual treatment for anxiety and to talk specifically about my combat experiences in Viet Nam. Experiences that I have yet to talk about in #Veteranslikeus: PTSD Symptoms In Combat Soldiers

I didn't know it was to be a time limited study of 44 sessions. Of the first two segments in the clinical study, 37 sessions covered effectively treating anxiety symptoms and 7 dealt with Viet Nam.

The third and final segment involved three evaluation interviews at 3, 6 and 12 months with the original therapist to find out how well you have done.

The anxiety portion went very well for me. Within weeks of starting the C-B-T, the therapist had me walking outside my house for the first time in literally 7 years. I started shopping in stores, going to restaurants and attending movies. My average sleeping hours per day decreased to 10 hours per day from a high of 16 hours. I began to take my medications on a regular basis.

I had every confidence in the therapist that we when moved to the Viet Nam portion of the study that I would also make significant healing of my experiences in Viet Nam.

The concept behind talking about my Viet Nam experiences is to tell what happened and what I was feeling as the event unfolded. This was to be recorded onto a tape cassette for me to listen to 2 or 3 times before the next session.

At which time, I would relive with the therapist the same combat experience over again in far greater detail than in the first tape. A third session on the same combat experience was to bring "closure"

At which point, the therapist and I would then move forward to the second combat experience and repeat the same procedure as in the first tape. And ultimately a third combat experience would unfold like the previous two events.

Except that this procedure did not work for me.

In fact, as I did the first tape and listened to the experience over and over, the symptoms of my PTSD (sadness, rage, anger, crying jags, irritability, nightmares, sweat soaked sheets, major league depression, I am even yelling at five year old Hailey) grew steadily worse until my brain said, in effect, "Don't do this process any more."

And as I started the second combat experience with the therapist, this is exactly what happened.

This resulted in the therapist and I not completing the procedures for a second or third Viet Nam combat experience. This left the therapist with no choice but to stop this portion of my individual treatment and move on to other VA psychological research projects.

With my PTSD symptoms firing on all cylinders, I am faced with the immediate necessity of finding another VA therapist to finish the work began by the original VA therapist.

At some point after treatment stopped, VA officials make an administrative decision that lets me know that I should be grateful to be invited to be included in two clinical studies for determining the best course of treatment for Viet Nam vets with severe PTSD and attending a weekly PTSD group at Ft. Miley.

((Even though I have been in the VA medical system for PTSD since 1989; until August of this year, I have never had an individual VA therapist specifically treat me for my Viet Nam experiences.

Until two months ago, my PTSD group would go for periods of up to nine weeks without the word "Viet Nam" being mentioned. Discussion centered on prescriptions, financial worries, physical ailments, family/friend relationships and current politicians.

Would a member of a support group for rape victims in which the word "rape" is not mentioned for weeks at a time and that discussion within the meeting center on prescriptions, past and current relationships or any other subject except for the one that brought them to the group ...continue to attend?

I doubt very much that meetings of Alcohol Anonymous go without mentioning the word "alcohol" for up to 9 weeks at a time.

Something is fundamentally wrong here! I can't speak for other VA PTSD groups across the country but if they are run the same way, then any combat veteran's expectations of discussing what happened to them while they were in Viet Nam won't happen and the treatment of convenience for VA officials will remain to medicate, medicate and medicate.

Perhaps, this is one of the reasons that the majority of PTSD veterans stay away from Veteran Affairs Medical Centers is because they see through the illusion of receiving serious help for their PTSD experiences.

My experience is that the veteran is never given the opportunity to regularly talk extensively about those experiences that brought him to the VA in the first place.

Because Ft. Miley is a teaching hospital for University of California –San Francisco medical school, the mental health services at Ft. Miley that treat veterans are divided into staff and interns. The medical interns are students who have their medical degree but are now in the second year (of three years) of training to become licensed California psychiatrists.

The other class of intern is the pre-doctoral psychology student who already has his/her baccalaureate degree. Typically, they come from UCSF for a six month period in the PTSD department and then rotate into other psychology departments (Gerontology or In-Patient care) at Ft. Miley. They are each supervised by the full time staff and do see individual PTSD clients. Currently, they must have 3000 hours of supervised internship before they get their license.

The problem with this is that by the time patient gets into a healing groove with this "intern", the six month period (if that) is over and it is time for the PTSD patient to wait for another "intern" to continue the treatment. And begin the process of starting from scratch ....again. Plus, this is usually the first time the "intern" gets to be involved with a patient in a non-academic setting.

We become their laboratory mice. As combat vets, we need more than just students learning their craft.

From talking to each member of my Monday PTSD group as well as selected members of the Tuesday weekly PTSD group, I discovered only one individual who has a full time Ft. Miley staff member doing his long term individual therapy.

The rest of us don't have a full time staff member or intern doing individual long term therapy with us.

For those who do have an individual therapist beyond the weekly group meetings, it is an intern with the emphasis on the here-and-now and not dealing with what happened 35 years ago.

I don't have to be a mental health expert to know that you don't just treat a wound by putting a dressing or topical ointment on the surface of the skin. If there is an infection lurking beneath the skin, it needs to be effectively dealt with by antibiotics or surgery. Our infection are our Vietnam experiences and worthy of professional medical treatment instead of a revolving door of students learning on the job.

I don't believe this is the fault of the individual therapist but rather the way the PTSD treatment programs are supervised by VA officials in Washington and Regional Offices across the country. It appears the emphasis is on "numbers" instead of what is best course of action in "restoring the patient to a healthy and productive quality of life."

It is not my job to lead, supervise or facilitate my PTSD group in bringing forth those individual Viet Nam memories that still cause significant distress. Somebody else gets paid to do this.))

Subsequent to the meeting among the four therapists, I am told that the chances of my getting a VA therapist to continue my therapy is not looking good due to budget cuts, staff shortages, influx of Gulf War veterans and furthermore I will have to be put on a long list of other veterans waiting for an individual therapist.

This decision means I will have to pay a private sector psychiatrist $150 per hour or more to continue where the original therapist left off.

This absolutely and positively enrages me as I remember experiences like that which began this edition of Season or Sorrows. Or other experiences in #Veteranslikeus: PTSD Symptoms In Combat Soldiers .

I sink into deep despair and despondency. It was bad enough fighting in Viet Nam. Now the US Government agency that got $72 billion dollars in 2005 to treat veterans like me ...won't go that extra mile to treat me successfully.

This is the lowest point in my life since I started anew with VA medications in 1997.

For several days, fleeting thoughts of suicide cross my mind and then pass. Something is fundamentally wrong when I can't get the psychological treatment I need from the VA.

The medications get me back on track and I decide that I am entitled to better psychological treatment than what I am getting.

So with Stephanie's help, I write a letter to the Patient Advocate at Ft. Miley outlining my outrage.

This leads to a one hour meeting (I am not present or invited) between four VA therapists to find a solution: i.e. a qualified VA therapist with formal training and experience in treating PTSD and available to treat me on an long term basis.

(A copy of this letter is available upon request.)

Ultimately, I am referred to a second VA therapist (in a non Ft. Miley location) with excellent credentials for treating my disorder. So far, I have had three meetings with this therapist within the past eight weeks as we begin the process of establishing a mutual comfort level necessary to reveal and heal those Viet Nam memories that haunt me today.

If I hadn't complained to the Patient Advocate, my current therapy would continue to be medications and weekly PTSD therapy sessions in which the word "Vietnam" and my (our) experiences there would not be talked about.

I am upset that any VA official can even hint/suggest/think that I should be grateful.

The combat experiences that I share from #Veteranslikeus: PTSD Symptoms In Combat Soldiers and others that I haven't/won't share from #Veteranslikeus: PTSD Symptoms In Combat Soldiers tell me unmistakably that I'm entitled to the best psychological help for whatever length of time necessary from the best licensed psychiatrists/psychologists that Ft. Miley can offer. I earned it ...the hard way.

The VA gets $72 billion a year to treat veterans like me.

Should I have further difficulty getting the psychological treatment that I need from the VA, I will ask the send them to individual members of both the House and Senate Committee for Appropriations/Veterans Affairs.

These elected officials need to directly ask VA officials as to "Why, with $72 billion dollars from Congress, should PTSD rated combat veterans from WWII, Korea, Granada, Viet Nam, Iraq and Afghanistan ever be faced with paying out-of-pocket for needed psychiatric services."

"Is it VA policy to treat chronic PTSD symptoms only with medications and/or weekly therapy groups?

"What happens when a severely impacted PTSD veteran at a Veterans Affairs Medical Center needs more help than the medications and/or weekly therapy groups allow?"

"What therapy program is now in place to effectively treat those chronic PTSD veterans unable to attend group meetings?"

These questions and more need to be asked by members of Congress; especially those U.S. Senators and U.S. Representatives, charged with approving the VA annual budget and should be answered from all levels of VA officials from Secretary for Veterans Affairs R. James Nicholson down to the Regional Level.

We are entitled to the best licensed psychological help available from the VA because each of us in our own way earned it ...the hard way.

And I do mean ...the hard way.

Just for the record, the combat experience listed at the beginning of this edition of #Veteranslikeus: PTSD Symptoms In Combat Soldiers was my first significant combat action in South Viet Nam; the first time I engaged in hand-to-hand combat; the first-and-only time I got a knife wound; and the fact, I had been in-country just over a week.

Until this past August, no VA therapist or intern at the Veterans Affairs Medical Center has ever asked me anything about my experiences in Viet Nam

And now, after five years of weekly PTSD group meetings, not one of the members knows of this experience until they read it here. I know even less of their combat experiences because members are not encouraged, urged, prodded, nudged or inspired to talk about what happened to them in Viet Nam.

Something is fundamentally wrong here!

(This rant ends with my absolute belief that each therapist I have encountered along the way has done the best they can within the limitations imposed by the VA. Several have gone the extra extra mile to get me the help I need. I know and they know who they are. I continue to be more than grateful for their warm, caring and professional concern for my well-being).

In a press release issued on November 10th 2005, R. James Nicholson, Secretary of Veteran Affairs stated: "We have a commitment to ensure veterans with PTSD receive compassionate, world-class health care and appropriate disability compensation".

I believe that I have certainly received compassionate and world class health care from the Ft. Miley emergency room, GI and Dental Clinic, Nurse-Practitioners as well as the Radiology and the Partial Hospitilization Program when I needed it.

There are approximately 26, 000,000 veterans eligible for healthcare from the Veterans Administration. Currently, the Veterans Administration has 7.500,000 enrollments.

But if the VA isn't going to effectively help the 72,000 disabled service connected veterans rated 100% disabled (like me) with the root cause of their disability, who is?

My brain is broken. And it wasn't that way when I went to Viet Nam.

Somebody in the VA or elsewhere needs to help me.

Please.

Sere

PS:
Words of wisdom: If the NVA can see you, you will soon be dead. If you can see the NVA, they will soon be dead because when the NVA are within range of your weapons, you are within the range of their weapons.

When You Cross Paths With A Lonely Veteran, Ask Them:

"Do You Feel You Have No One To Talk To?"

"Do You Feel All Alone In Meeting Your Daily Challenges?"

"Have You Recently Lost Anybody Important In Your Life?"

And if you feel like you want to help improve the quality of life for a lonely, visit https://companions.lpages.co/many-veterans-have-no-friends/ **to see how you can help ...**

www.ingramcontent.com/pod-product-compliance
Lightning Source LLC
Chambersburg PA
CBHW072105280526
45788CB00006B/2408